Gathered from the Garden

Quilts with Floral Charm

CINDY LAMMON

Martingale®
& COMPANY

Gathered from the Garden: Quilts with Floral Charm
© 2008 by Cindy Lammon

That Patchwork Place® is an imprint of
Martingale & Company®.

Martingale & Company
20205 144th Ave. NE
Woodinville, WA 98072-8478 USA
www.martingale-pub.com

Credits

President & CEO » Tom Wierzbicki
Publisher » Jane Hamada
Editorial Director » Mary V. Green
Managing Editor » Tina Cook
Technical Editor » Darra Williamson
Copy Editor » Melissa Bryan
Design Director » Stan Green
Production Manager » Regina Girard
Illustrator » Adrienne Smitke
Cover & Text Designer » Stan Green
Photographer » Brent Kane

MISSION STATEMENT
Dedicated to providing quality products
and service to inspire creativity.

Printed in China
13 12 11 10 09 08   8 7 6 5 4 3 2 1

Library of Congress Cataloging-in-Publication Data
Library of Congress Control Number: 2008006216

ISBN: 978-1-56477-813-0

DEDICATION

In memory of my grandmother, Mildred Willig, a master seamstress and, to my knowledge, the first quilter in my family.

ACKNOWLEDGMENTS

One thing I know for sure is that nothing is accomplished alone. Special thanks to:

Martingale & Company for being a pleasure to work with and for publishing such beautiful books.

Ann Hazelwood and all the girls at Patches Etc. Quilt Shop for the inspiration and encouragement.

Marilyn Webert, not only a great quilting friend but a great friend, for introducing me to freezer paper for appliqué.

"The Girls"—Jean Maiuro, Wynema Bean, Cindy Black, and Pam Brown—for their continuous support, and for just wanting to have fun!

My children, Andrea and Bryan, who claim they've spent half their childhoods waiting in quilt shops.

My husband, Mike, for being a great provider, not only of love and support, but of lots of comic relief!

Contents

Page 23

Page 33

Page 37

Page 41

Page 51

Page 65

Page 69

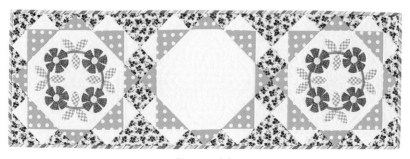

Page 44

Introduction

ARE YOU A QUILTER WHO ALSO LOVES TO GARDEN? MANY OF US DO, AND EVEN THOSE OF US WHO ARE NOT BLESSED WITH A GREEN THUMB TYPICALLY LOVE AND APPRECIATE BEAUTIFUL GARDENS.

CREATING AN EYE-CATCHING GARDEN takes the same creativity and attention to color and texture that we use in designing our quilts. At the nursery, I often find myself choosing plants by looking at their combinations of color, leaf patterns, size, and scale. Sound familiar? It's no wonder that quilting and gardening go hand in hand. I hope you'll find that the projects in this book add elements of nature to your quilts through the use of floral fabric, appliqué, color, and texture.

In fact, my idea for this book began in the garden. As I looked with amazement at the beauty of the flowers, I simply had to find a way to bring them indoors—and quilting them seemed the obvious answer. Why not just appliqué them onto a quilt or table runner? I'd never need to worry about watering!

Don't you love those gardens where at every turn you discover something new? You may find a bold burst of color, a quiet place to sit, or a bird's nest tucked away in a sheltered corner. You'll have just as much fun making these quilts. "My Secret Garden" (page 69), for example, in which each block is a new creative endeavor, offers many opportunities to play with color and texture as you stitch.

And—of course!—who can resist those gorgeous floral fabrics in the shops today? Mix a great floral print, some plaids, stripes, and floral coordinates, and you'll be on your way to a great pieced, garden-themed quilt. We are so lucky to have such wonderful and colorful floral fabrics. Don't pass up the chance to use them!

Finally, inspiration is just outside your window! Use these patterns as shown or explore your own ideas for adding nature to your bedding, pillows, tables, and walls. Bring a garden into your home and I hope, on a cold winter's day, your quilts will warm your heart!

Quiltmaking Basics

In the following pages, you'll find the basics for making your own garden-inspired projects. Hand-appliqué techniques, which I used for many of the projects in this book, are covered in detail in a separate section (page 17).

SELECTING FABRIC

Traditionally, quilts have been made with 100%-cotton fabrics. Cottons come in beautiful colors and are readily available for today's quilters. Choose good-quality cotton and you'll have material that is wonderful to work with and will last for generations to come.

I recommend prewashing all your cotton quilting fabric before you use it. Washing shrinks the fabric, removes any excess dyes, and makes the fabric soft and easy to work with, especially for appliqué. If you want to restore the finish that washing removes, spray your fabric with sizing or starch before you cut into it.

When I start a quilt, the first thing I do is decide on a color scheme. Inspiration may come from a picture, something in your home, a particular fabric, or directly from nature. Once you've established the color scheme, it's time to go shopping!

Choose fabrics in your color range, but more important, be sure there is some contrast in value between the fabrics. In most cases, you don't want your fabrics to visually blend. As you do your piecing and appliqué, you want the design to emerge. That means putting light fabrics next to mediums or darks. Without contrast, the design may be lost in your finished quilt!

After color and contrast, make sure that you have a variety of textures in your fabrics—an element often overlooked by quilters, as many of us concentrate primarily on color. Texture here refers to the fabric's *visual* texture (or print). Look for prints with different motifs, such as paisleys, dots, plaids, flowers, vines, lines, and swirls. Including fabrics with several different textures will prevent your quilt from looking "flat."

Finally, make sure to choose fabrics that represent a variety of print sizes. Include large-, medium-, and small-scale prints to keep your quilt looking interesting.

Once you've made all the fabric selections for your quilt, step back and look at them from a distance. We tend to look at our fabrics close up on the bolt, but chances are your finished quilt will be viewed from a distance, on the bed or on the wall. Set the bolts upright and step back to visualize how the fabrics will look together. Consider color, contrast, texture, and size of print to find a winning combination.

To create the garden-themed quilts in this book, look for prints that remind you of nature, flowers, leaves, and gardens in both color and texture. Create a garden style by pairing floral prints generously with plaids, stripes, checks, and leaf designs. Use nature as your inspiration and you'll create a quilt that has the warmth and beauty of the outdoors.

ROTARY CUTTING

Rotary cutting is not only a quick method of cutting multiple pieces, but also a very accurate one. You'll need a rotary cutter, a self-healing mat that measures at least 24" in one direction, and an acrylic ruler at least 24" long. A second acrylic ruler in a smaller, square size (such as a Bias Square®) also comes in handy for cleaning up fabric edges when cutting strips, trimming half-square-triangle units to size, and cutting small pieces.

The following instructions are for right-handed quilters. Reverse if you are left-handed.

1. Press your fabric and fold it as it comes off the bolt—that is, with the selvages aligned. Place the fabric on the cutting mat with the folded edge closest to you. Position the bulk of the fabric to your right, so you will be cutting on the left edge.

2. The first cut is called a "cleanup cut" since it removes the fabric's ragged edges and squares the cut edge to the fold of the fabric. This is an important step: if your cuts are not made at a right angle to the fold, the strips will not be straight when you unfold them. To square the fabric, align a small, square ruler along the folded edge. Place a large ruler to the left, butting it up against the small ruler as shown.

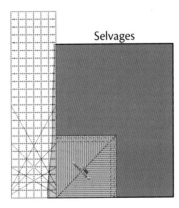

Selvages

3. Remove the small ruler and cut along the right edge of the large ruler as shown.

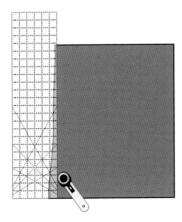

4. To cut strips, position the large ruler so the desired measurement is aligned with the newly cut edge of the fabric. I like to place a horizontal line of the ruler along the fold of the fabric to be sure that my fabric remains squared. If you find that the ruler has slipped, and you are no longer square to the fold, repeat steps 1–3 to make another cleanup cut.

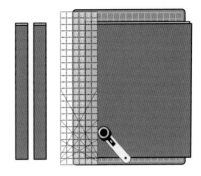

5. Once you've cut the fabric into strips, you can crosscut the strips into squares or rectangles. Place a strip horizontally on the cutting mat. Trim off the selvages and square up the end of the strip with a cleanup cut. Align the desired measurement on your ruler with the newly trimmed edge of the fabric, and proceed to cut the strip into the required number of squares or rectangles.

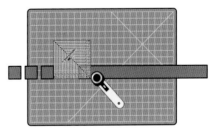

6. To rotary cut triangles, first cut squares from strips, and then cut the squares either once or twice on the diagonal. Both result in 90° (right-angle) triangles, but with the stretchy bias grain on different edges. A half-square triangle (one diagonal cut) has the bias on the long diagonal

edge. A quarter-square triangle (two diagonal cuts) has the bias on the two short, right-angled sides.

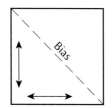
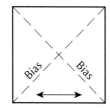

Half-square triangles. Straight of grain on the two short sides.

Quarter-square triangles. Straight of grain on the long side.

Since bias edges are so stretchy, it is better to have the straight of grain on the outside edges of the finished block whenever possible; this placement dictates whether the project instructions direct you to cut half-square or quarter-square triangles.

FOR BEST RESULTS

When cutting squares into triangles, make the diagonal cuts immediately after cutting the proper-sized squares. This is particularly important if you are cutting multiple layers of fabric. Moving the squares and cutting them later can cause the fabric layers to shift, resulting in inaccurately cut triangles.

MACHINE PIECING

The patterns in this book are based on sewing with a ¼"-wide seam allowance. The accuracy and consistency of your seam will directly affect how the segments of the blocks fit together and how the blocks fit together into the quilt. You can save yourself lots of frustration later by taking the time *now* to be certain your ¼" seam allowance is true.

To do this, you'll need a guide on your sewing machine. Many machines have a special piecing foot that measures exactly ¼" from the edge of the foot to the needle. If you don't have a special foot, create a guide on the bed of the machine by using a small ruler to measure ¼" from the needle and

placing a piece of masking tape at this spot on the throat plate.

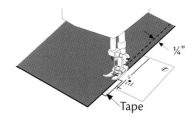

Tape

Once you've established a ¼" guide, I recommend doing a quick test to be sure you are getting accurate results. It is more important for the piece you are stitching to measure the proper size when finished than for the seam allowance to measure ¼". In fact, most quilters find that a scant ¼" (a few threads less than ¼") gives the best result since a few threads are lost in the fold when the sewn seams are pressed.

To test your seam allowance, cut three 1½" x 3" strips of fabric. With right sides together, sew the strips together along the long edges. Carefully press the seam allowances to one side. The resulting unit should measure exactly 3½" across its width. If your unit does not measure 3½", make some adjustments in your stitching and try again. For a unit that is too small, take a slightly smaller seam allowance. If the unit is too big, make your seam allowance a little bigger.

3½"

When machine piecing, you must also be mindful of bias edges. Bias edges are created when the fabric is cut at any angle other than 90°. Fabric cut at a 45° angle is cut on the "true bias."

All triangles have at least one edge that is a bias edge. The bias is quite stretchy, and your piece can be pulled out of shape easily when you sew on this edge. Be aware when you are sewing a seam that involves a bias edge, being very careful not to pull on it and stretch it as you sew. Simply let the machine guide the fabric under the needle while maintaining the ¼" seam allowance. With just a bit of attention, your triangles will always look like triangles!

PRESSING

In quilting, seam allowances are generally pressed to one side. Once a seam is sewn, place the unit on the ironing board and press the seam flat from the wrong side with a hot, dry iron. Next, open the unit and press the seam in the desired direction from the right side, with the edge of the iron along the seam line. Hold the iron in place; too much movement can distort the pieces. Pressing from the right side in this manner prevents tucks from forming at the seam line.

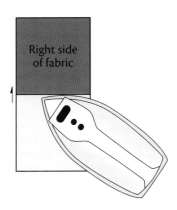

Several factors determine the direction in which to press the seam allowances. The most important factor is related to the construction of the block. When two seams meet, pressing the seam allowances in opposite directions not only reduces the bulk, but also allows the seams to "nest," helping you to match the intersections perfectly.

Opposing seams

When a seam does not intersect another seam, I like to press the seam allowance the easy way—in whichever direction it wants to go! This is often away from points and results in a nice, flat seam and crisp points.

If construction and ease of pressing are not factors, I generally press the seam allowance toward the darker fabric. This assures that the darker fabric will not show through the lighter one.

Despite what you may have heard, seams *can* be pressed open. I often do this when there are many seams coming together, which creates a great deal of bulk. Simply open the seam and press it flat.

To help you, each project includes pressing instructions, either in the text or with arrows in the accompanying diagrams. If no pressing direction is indicated, seams can be pressed in any direction.

When the block is complete, I like to use steam in my iron to give the block a final press. The block can also be misted with water and pressed flat. Flat blocks result in flat quilts, so this is a good step to take.

STRIP PIECING

Several patterns in this book use strip-piecing techniques to quickly and accurately construct multiple identical units. To strip piece, cut long strips across the width of the fabric in the width and length described in the project instructions. With right sides together, sew the strips together along the long edges as instructed and press.

Once the strip set is assembled, treat it as one piece of fabric. Place the strip set horizontally on your cutting mat and do a cleanup cut to trim the selvages and square the end (page 9). Crosscut the strip set into segments of the required size and number.

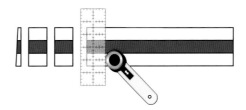

FOLDED TRIANGLES

This method of sewing triangles at the corners of other shapes eliminates the need for cutting oddly shaped pieces and dealing with bias edges. No triangles are involved. The units are constructed from a large square or rectangle and smaller squares that are cleverly transformed into triangles in the finished piece.

1. Use a sharp pencil and a ruler to draw a diagonal line from corner to corner on the wrong side of the small squares as instructed.

    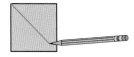

2. With right sides together, place a marked square on the appropriate corner of the larger base piece, making sure to note the direction of the drawn line. Sew directly on the diagonal line.

    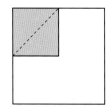

3. Fold the small square along the seam toward the outer edge of the unit and press. The edges of the small folded square should match the edges of the base piece. Carefully trim the two bottom layers, leaving a ¼" seam allowance.

    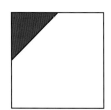 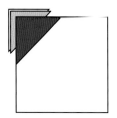

ASSEMBLING THE QUILT

Use the quilt assembly diagram, included with the project instructions, to arrange the completed blocks in a pleasing manner. Placing them on a wall-mounted flannel board is a great way to get a clear picture of how your finished quilt will look. If possible, step back from the blocks and view them from a distance to make sure the overall design is balanced and that your eye is not drawn and held by one particular area.

Sew the blocks (and sashing, if applicable) together in rows. Press the seam allowances for each row in the opposite direction from the previous row. This makes it easier to match the seams when you are sewing the rows together. I like to sew the rows together in pairs, then sew the pairs together into sections of four rows, and so on, until I have assembled the quilt in two halves that I join to complete the quilt center. This method allows for minimal handling of the entire large quilt top at the sewing machine.

Adding the Borders

The border strips for a quilt can be cut from either the crosswise (selvage to selvage) or lengthwise (parallel to the selvage) grain of the fabric. Cutting strips from the crosswise grain generally requires less fabric, but the strips must be sewn together to get the required length, resulting in a seam on the border. I like to save fabric, so I cut my borders on the crosswise grain unless the fabric is a large print or plaid and the seam will be obvious.

To finish with a quilt that is flat and squared at the corners, your borders must be of equal length on opposite sides. If a quilt is even ½" larger on one side than the opposite side, it is no longer a truly square or rectangular quilt. Since the edges of the quilt center may not be the exact same measurement once the blocks are sewn together, attaching a border and then trimming it almost *guarantees* that the lengths of the opposite borders are not the same.

You can measure across your quilt center and cut the two opposite borders to that measurement, but since it is so easy to make mistakes in measuring, I use the following method to trim my borders to length instead. You've probably heard the saying

"Measure twice, cut once." I have found that a better solution is not to measure at all.

1. Piece the border strips together end to end, if necessary, to create two borders that are several inches longer than the sides of the quilt. Place the quilt top flat on a table or on the floor and layer the two border strips down the center of the quilt. Use a rotary cutter, ruler, and cutting mat to trim the borders even with the raw edges of the quilt. You now have two border strips that are equal to each other and to the quilt without having taken any measurements!

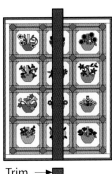

Trim. →

2. Find the center points of the border strips and the quilt center by folding them in half and marking with a pin. Place one border strip on each side of the quilt, matching the ends and the center points. Pin the borders in place and sew them to the body of the quilt. You may need to ease the border strips or the quilt center a bit to make them fit, but it's easy to do so over this long side of the quilt. In most cases, you will want to press the seam allowances toward the border.

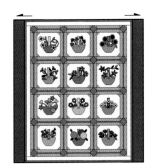

3. Repeat step 1 with the top and bottom borders, placing them across the center of the quilt and trimming them even with the raw edges of the quilt top, which now includes the side borders. Sew these borders to the top and bottom edges of the quilt. I like to take a few backstitches on these last two seams of the quilt to prevent the seam from coming apart during quilting.

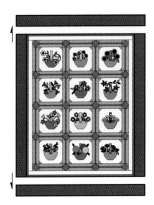

FINISHING TECHNIQUES

Plan for the backing for your quilt to measure approximately 4" larger than the quilt top in both directions to allow for shifting in the layering and basting stages. If your quilt top is larger than 36", you will need to piece the backing to accommodate the quilt's size. Press the seam of the backing fabric open to avoid having a lump down the center of the quilt.

Layering and Basting

Press the quilt top and the backing fabric well. If you need to mark any quilting designs, do so after the final pressing, but before the quilt is layered. For machine quilting, I use small, rustproof quilter's safety pins to baste the quilt. For hand quilting, I like to thread baste. For either method, the layering is the same.

Place the backing fabric flat, wrong side up, on a table or on the floor. Pull the backing taut without stretching it, and secure it well all the way around with masking tape (or pins). Center and spread the batting over the backing, matching the centers and smoothing out any wrinkles. Place the quilt top over the batting, right side up, centering it and gently smoothing it with your hands to feel for any bumps or folds.

Using either thread or safety pins, baste the quilt in a grid with horizontal and vertical lines spaced 3" to 4" apart.

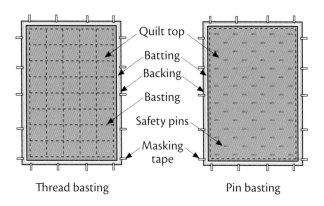

Thread basting   Pin basting

Quilting

Both hand quilting and machine quilting work beautifully on any of these quilts. Here are some things to keep in mind so that the quilting enhances your piecing and appliqué.

- Keep the density of the quilting fairly even over the surface of the quilt. Combining areas of heavy quilting with areas of sparse quilting will result in a quilt that does not lie flat.
- Use a combination of geometric and curvy motifs in the quilt for added interest.
- Quilt the background of appliqué designs to make the appliqué "pop."
- Thread color is very important. Quilting thread that matches the fabric color blends into the fabric and simply creates contour. Thread in a highly contrasting color stands out to become an additional design element.

Squaring Up

Once the quilting is finished, the edges of the quilt may be a little uneven. Use your rotary cutter and ruler to trim the borders of the quilt so they are

straight and even and to square the corners. You will be trimming the backing and batting even with the quilt top at the same time in preparation for the binding.

Binding

I like to use a French double-fold binding on my quilts. This folded binding is easy to apply and gives a double layer of fabric that wears well. I generally cut the binding strips 2½" wide, but they can be slightly narrower or wider depending on the desired look. Yardage calculations for binding the quilts in this book are based on 2½"-wide strips.

The binding strips can be cut on the straight grain or on the bias. For straight-grain binding, recommended for most quilts in this book, cut the strips across the fabric width, from selvage to selvage. I like to cut the binding on the bias when I'm using a striped, a checked, or a plaid fabric because I like the look of the diagonal line around the edge of the quilt. "Garden Wreath Table Runner" (page 44) features bias binding cut from a striped fabric, "Gathered from the Garden Wall Hanging" (page 33) features bias binding cut from a checked fabric, and "Down the Garden Path" (page 65) features bias binding cut from a plaid fabric; I've given yardage and cutting instructions for both straight-grain and bias strips for these projects so that you can choose either option.

1. Cut enough strips so that you have a length equal to the perimeter of the quilt plus 10". To cut strips on the straight grain, refer to "Rotary Cutting," steps 1–4 (page 9). To cut bias strips, open the fabric to one layer and press it flat. Place the fabric on your cutting mat and position your long acrylic ruler on the fabric so that the ruler's 45° line is on the fabric's selvage edge. Cut along the edge of the

ruler to establish the 45° angle, and—from the newly angled edge—cut as many 2½" strips as required. Trim the ends of the strips square.

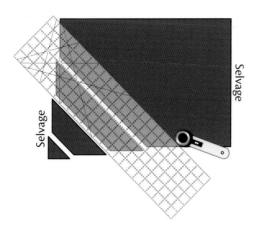

2. Place the ends of two strips (either straight-grain or bias) right sides together at right angles, and use your preferred marker to draw a diagonal line as shown. Sew directly on the line. Add the remaining strips in the same manner, trim the seam allowances to ¼", and press the seams open.

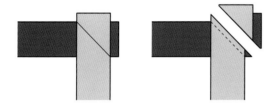

3. Fold the strip in half lengthwise with wrong sides together and press.

4. Place the raw edges of the binding strip even with the raw edge of the quilt. Using a walking foot if possible, begin sewing the binding to the quilt with a ¼" seam allowance, leaving about 10" free at the starting end. Sew to the first corner, stopping ¼" from the corner; backstitch.

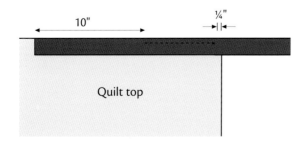

10"   ¼"

Quilt top

5. To miter the corner, remove the quilt from the machine and turn the quilt so you are ready to begin sewing the binding to the second side. Fold the binding up at a 45° angle, even with the next side of the quilt.

6. Fold the binding back down, aligning the fold with the top raw edge of the quilt and the raw edges of the binding with the raw edge of the quilt's second side. Beginning at the fold, resume sewing the binding to the quilt, mitering each corner as you come to it.

7. Stop sewing about 10" before you reach the starting tail of the binding. Place the quilt on a flat surface and overlap the two ends of the binding strips. Trim the overlap equal to the original cut width of the binding, which in this case is 2½".

2½" overlap

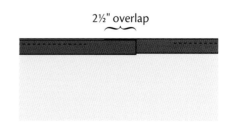

8. Place the beginning and ending tails right sides together at right angles and draw a diagonal line as you did in step 2. Pin, and stitch on the line.

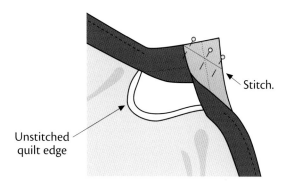

Unstitched quilt edge

Stitch.

9. Check the binding to be sure it fits. Trim the seam allowance to ¼" and finger-press it open. Refold the binding, pin it in place, and finish stitching it to the quilt.

10. Fold the binding over the edge of the quilt to the back. Blindstitch the binding to the quilt back using a thread color that matches the binding. Miters will form at the corners.

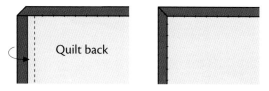

Quilt back

Hand-Appliqué Techniques

MOST QUILTERS HAVE A FAVORITE APPLIQUÉ METHOD, AND I'M NO DIFFERENT. IN THIS SECTION I EXPLAIN THE TECHNIQUES THAT I PREFER BECAUSE THEY PRODUCE EXCELLENT RESULTS FOR ME. TRY THESE METHODS, OR USE YOUR FAVORITE MEANS OF APPLIQUÉ TO COMPLETE THE PROJECTS IN THE BOOK.

PREPARING THE BACKGROUND

As you appliqué, the edges of the background block sometimes get frayed or pulled out of shape, so cut the background fabric 1" to 1½" larger than the finished block. When the appliqué is complete, you can trim your block to the proper size.

Establish centering lines by folding the background block in half vertically and finger-pressing the crease. Open the block and fold it in half again, this time horizontally, and finger-crease. Never use an iron to press these creases, as this may make them difficult to remove later.

Use one or a combination of the following methods to prepare the background for positioning the appliqué pieces.

The No-Mark Method

When designs are free form and the appliqué pieces do not need to be placed symmetrically on the background, you can simply use the photo or appliqué placement diagram as a guide to arrange the appliqués in a pleasing manner. If certain elements of the design need to be centered, use the centering creases on the block for guidance. This no-mark method saves time and involves no marked lines on the background that may not be covered by the appliqué later.

The Marked-Background Method

When appliqué pieces must be placed symmetrically on the background, or when you wish to duplicate the pattern *exactly*, you will need to mark the appliqué layout on the background block. In many cases, you need to mark only a portion of the design. For example, I often mark only the stems, and I position the flowers and leaves using the no-mark method described at left. Whether you mark the entire design or just a few key guidelines, the trick is to place the markings where they will be completely covered by your appliqué pieces.

You'll need a light box in order to trace the pattern onto the background. You can purchase a light box, build your own, or place a light source beneath a clear glass table or large plastic box. Secure the pattern to the light box and position your background fabric on top, centering the pattern by using the creases in the background block for guidance.

Use a pencil to mark the pattern on the fabric. It's important to mark as lightly as possible, and to keep the markings inside the pattern lines. This ensures that the markings will be covered by the appliqués and will not show when the appliqué is complete. For example, I like to mark a single line down the center to indicate the placement of a stem; this way, the appliquéd stem will completely cover the marking.

Mark the placement of leaves, flowers, and other pieces with positioning marks ⅛" *inside* the pattern line. It's not always necessary to trace the entire shape. A piece such as a leaf will need only a few guide marks at each end. This keeps the marking to a minimum, but still ensures proper positioning of the appliqué shape.

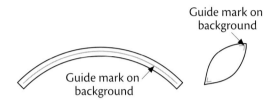

Guide mark on background

Guide mark on background

The Overlay Method

I use the overlay method when I'm appliquéing a flower with multiple petals. It ensures that each petal will be positioned properly in relation to the other petals. This technique is also helpful when you are using a dark background and it's not easy to see through the fabric to trace the markings onto the background.

Draw the design, such as the individual flower, onto clear plastic (I like to cut up plastic page protectors for this purpose) or tracing paper. Position the overlay on top of the background block, slip the individual pieces under the overlay into position on the background, and pin the appliqués in place.

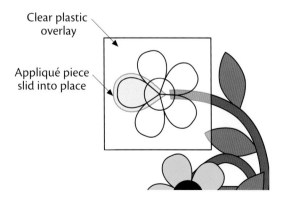

Clear plastic overlay

Appliqué piece slid into place

PREPARING THE APPLIQUÉ PIECES

For most shapes, such as flowers and leaves, I use freezer paper for my appliqué templates. The waxy (shiny) side of the paper can be ironed onto the fabric and removed cleanly when the stitching is completed. I use my needle to turn under the seam allowance as I appliqué. Some shapes, such as stems and circles, require different handling. More on this later.

GOING IN REVERSE!

For any asymmetrical pattern piece, you will need to make the freezer-paper pattern in reverse so that the appliqué will be oriented correctly when you stitch it to the background fabric. Of the dozens and dozens of pattern pieces in this book, only a few are asymmetrical, and in each case, the piece is identified on the pattern page with instructions for how to trace it. How easy is that?!

The overwhelming majority of pattern pieces are symmetrical and you don't need to worry about a thing. No matter how you trace them, these pieces are always "headed in the right direction."

Freezer-Paper Appliqué

1. Trace the appliqué shape onto the paper (dull) side of the freezer paper. Cut out the template directly on the drawn line. You can cut multiple layers by stapling several pieces of freezer paper together.

2. Press the waxy side of the freezer paper to the wrong side of the desired fabric with a dry iron. Leave approximately ¼" for seam allowance around each piece. Place curved edges on the bias when possible as this will make it easier to turn under the edges.

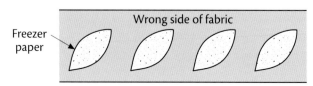

Wrong side of fabric

Freezer paper

3. Cut out each shape leaving a scant ¼" seam allowance.

TRY SPRAY STARCH

For appliqué pieces with straight edges, I like to press the seam allowance under using the freezer-paper template as a guide. This is easy to do and makes needle-turn appliqué go more quickly. To get a nice crisp edge, put a little starch on the seam allowance before pressing. Simply spray some starch into a cup or the lid of the can and use a small paintbrush to apply the starch to the seam allowance. Turn the seam allowance over the edge of the template with your finger and press with an iron until the fabric is completely dry.

Stems

Stems that curve must be cut on the bias of the fabric to have the necessary stretch. If the stems are straight, cut them on the straight grain so they remain straight as you appliqué them.

To cut bias strips, place the fabric on your cutting mat and position your acrylic ruler on the fabric so that the ruler's 45° line is on the fabric's selvage edge. Cut along the edge of the ruler to establish the 45° angle, and—from the newly angled edge—cut as many ⅞"-wide strips as required. If necessary, join strips to achieve the desired length. Press the seam allowances open.

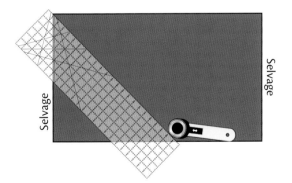

Cut straight strips along the straight grain of the fabric as usual. If strips must be pieced to reach the desired length, join at right angles as shown. Trim the seam allowance to ¼"; press open.

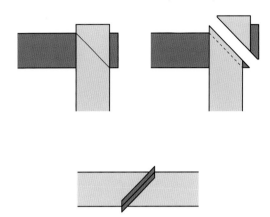

Whether you are using strips cut on the bias or on the straight grain, press about one-third of the strip width (in the case of a ⅞"-wide strip, a little more than ¼") to the wrong side along one long edge as shown. Fold the remaining long edge in the same way, and baste it in place using long basting stitches. The stem is now its finished width and ready to appliqué.

Circles

Circles more than 2" in diameter can be prepared by using a freezer-paper template as described in "Freezer-Paper Appliqué" (page 18). Circles smaller than 2" in diameter are difficult to needle turn, and can be made by using a template cut to the exact size of the required circle from cardboard or heat-resistant template plastic. You can purchase precut heat-resistant circle templates at many quilt shops and via the Internet. These handy notions come in many sizes and can be used over and over again.

Cut the fabric about ½" larger than the circle template to create a ¼" seam allowance. Sew a small gathering stitch around the outside edge of the fabric circle, within the ¼" seam allowance. Place the circle template in the center of the wrong side of the fabric circle and begin to gently pull up the gathering stitches. See the tip "Try Spray Starch" (page 19) and use a small paintbrush to apply starch to the gathered seam allowance.

Pull the fabric tight around the circle and press with an iron until the starch is completely dry. Turn the circle over to the right side and press again; loosen the gathering stitches and remove the plastic. If necessary, pull the gathering thread lightly to re-form the circle, and then clip off the thread. The edges of the circle are perfectly turned and the piece is ready to appliqué.

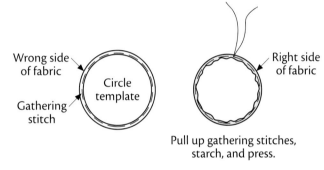

Wrong side of fabric

Gathering stitch

Circle template

Right side of fabric

Pull up gathering stitches, starch, and press.

STITCHING THE APPLIQUÉS

Once the background and the appliqué pieces are prepared, it's time to sew! I use a technique called "needle-turn" appliqué, in which the sewing needle is used to turn under the seam allowance on the edge of the piece. The best thread to use for hand appliqué is a fine silk thread in a color to match your appliqué piece; the silk will "melt" into your fabric and virtually disappear. Fine cotton thread is my second choice.

You'll also want to choose a good-quality needle for hand appliqué. I use a size 10 or 11 straw needle—a long, strong needle that works well for turning under seam allowances.

Finally, you'll need pins to hold the appliqué pieces in place. Short appliqué pins work better than long pins, which tend to catch the thread as you're sewing.

With a few rare exceptions, you'll work from the "bottom up" in placing and appliquéing the pattern pieces; in other words, a piece partially hidden beneath another shape is appliquéd first. Dotted lines on the patterns indicate where pieces overlap. Position the first piece and pin it in place. I like to place several small pins in the seam allowance around the piece. With pieces adhered to freezer-paper templates, you can peek underneath the fabric to see if the template is positioned exactly where you want it.

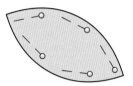

1. Unless you've pressed the edge under in preparing the piece, use your needle to turn the seam under where you want to start sewing. (The freezer paper on the wrong side provides a guide for the edge and prevents you from turning under too much seam allowance.) Hold the seam allowance in place with your non-sewing hand. Bring your needle up from the back, through the background and through the fold on the edge of the appliqué piece. Take your needle back down into the background only, at exactly the point where it came up through the fold of the appliqué. Move the needle horizontally along the wrong side of the background fabric, and come up about 1/16" from the previous stitch, through the background and the fold on the edge of the appliqué.

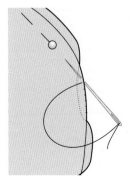

2. Continue stitching along the piece, holding the appliqué with your non-sewing hand and turning the seam allowance under with the needle as you go. You do not need to turn under edges that will be overlapped by another appliqué piece; these raw edges will be covered by the overlap. Finish stitching each piece by making a few backstitches on the back.

3. Remove freezer-paper templates by carefully cutting a slit on the wrong side of the background fabric behind the appliqué. Be careful to cut only the background fabric and not through the freezer paper. If you wish, you can cut out the background fabric, leaving a ¼" seam allowance inside the appliqué stitches. Gently tug on the freezer paper to loosen it and remove it.

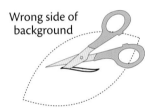

Wrong side of background

Pieces with inside curves need to be clipped in order for the seam allowance to turn smoothly. Use sharply pointed scissors to make several clips along the curve, about halfway into the seam allowance. The sharper the curve, the more clips you will need.

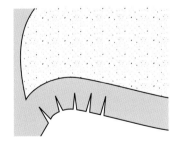

Make sharp outside points by stitching right up to the point and taking a stitch exactly at the point. Trim any excess seam allowance that peeks out the other side as shown. Turn the seam allowance

under at the point and then turn under the edge along the next side of the shape. Take a small tug on the thread, which will pull the point out sharply. Hold the piece with your non-sewing hand and continue sewing the next side.

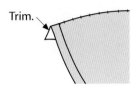

Trim.

Clip inside points three or four threads short of the freezer-paper template. When your stitching approaches the point, use your needle in a "sweeping" motion to turn under the seam allowance along the edge. Continue stitching until you reach the point, and then take a slightly deeper stitch of three or four threads. Bring your needle back into the background, slightly under your appliqué piece, and pull the needle through from the back. This motion will tuck under those three or four threads at the point. Bring the needle back up through the background and into the fold of the appliqué, and continue stitching as usual.

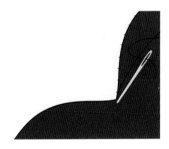

Make 1 stitch, 3–4 threads deep.

When all the appliqué on your block is complete, place the block right side down on a fluffy terry-cloth towel and press using a bit of steam. The plush towel keeps the appliqué from flattening out. Finish by trimming the block as directed—that is, to the finished size plus the seam allowance.

Pieced and appliquéd by Cindy Lammon. Machine quilted by Wanda Salzman.

Finished Quilt: 66½" x 82" • Finished Block: 12" x 12"

Gathered from the Garden

A BASKET OF FLOWERS GATHERED FROM THE GARDEN IS SUCH A BEAUTIFUL SIGHT . . .
JUST AS YOUR QUILT WILL BE WHEN YOUR BASKETS ARE FILLED WITH FLORAL APPLIQUÉ.

MATERIALS

*All yardages are based on 42"-wide fabric
unless otherwise noted. Fat quarters measure
18" x 21".*

2⅛ yards of red floral print for outer border
and binding

2 yards of cream tone-on-tone print for
block backgrounds and inner border

1⅞ yards of tan print for block corners,
sashing, and cornerstones

1⅛ yards of dark green print for sashing,
cornerstones, and middle border

⅞ yard *total* of assorted tan prints for
basket and basket handle appliqués

4 fat quarters of assorted green fabrics (or
equivalent scraps) for stem and leaf
appliqués

Assorted scraps of yellow, gold, black,
brown, red, and blue prints for flower
appliqués

5 yards of backing fabric

71" x 86" piece of batting

12 buttons, ½" to ⅝" in diameter

CUTTING

*Cut all strips across the width of the fabric unless
otherwise noted.*

From the cream tone-on-tone print, cut:
4 strips, 13" x 42"; crosscut into 12 squares, 13" x 13"
7 strips, 2" x 42"

From the *straight grain* of the 4 fat quarters of
assorted green fabrics, cut:
Enough ⅞"-wide strips to total approximately 45"

From the *bias* of the 4 fat quarters of assorted
green fabrics, cut:
Enough ⅞"-wide strips to total approximately 125"

From the tan print for sashing, cut:
7 strips, 2" x 42"; crosscut into 128 squares, 2" x 2"
22 strips, 2" x 42"

From the dark green print, cut:
3 strips, 4" x 42"; crosscut into 20 squares, 4" x 4"
11 strips, 1" x 42"
7 strips, 1½" x 42"

From the red floral print, cut:
8 strips, 6" x 42"
8 strips, 2½" x 42"

APPLIQUÉING THE BLOCKS

Refer to "Hand-Appliqué Techniques" (page 17) for guidance as needed.

For the blocks in this quilt, I recommend that you begin with the basket and basket handle appliqués, even though some stems and leaves are overlapped by the basket pieces. It just feels more natural to "arrange" the flowers with the baskets already in place.

1. Fold each 13" cream square in half in both directions and finger-crease to establish centering lines.

2. Use the patterns on page 27 and the assorted tan prints to prepare 12 basket and 12 basket handle appliqués. Referring to the tip box "Try Spray Starch" (page 19), press under the seam allowance on the long straight edge at the top of the basket and the straight edges of the handle.

3. Position a basket and basket handle on each 13" cream square. Position the basket so that the folded edge at the top of the basket is on the center horizontal crease and the basket is centered side to side as shown. Appliqué the sides and bottom of the basket, leaving the top edge free for now. Appliqué the handle, centering it on the vertical crease and placing the bottom edge 1" below the top edge of the basket.

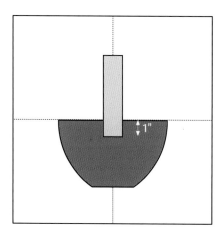

4. Referring to "Stems" (page 19), use the ⅞"-wide assorted green strips to prepare the required length of straight-grain and bias stems as described in the cutting list (page 23). As you make the blocks, you will cut curved stems from the prepared bias strips and straight stems from the prepared straight-grain strips.

5. Working one block at a time, use the pattern pieces on pages 28–31 and the assorted yellow, gold, black, brown, red, and blue scraps to prepare the flower appliqués (that is, the petals and flower centers) for each block. From the remaining assorted green prints, prepare the leaf appliqués for each block. The patterns tell you how many to cut of each piece, and how to deal with any reversed pieces. Refer to the photo on page 22 for color guidance as needed.

STAY ORGANIZED

To keep the many appliqué pieces for this quilt organized, place the pieces for each block in a separate resealable plastic bag labeled with the block name or number. This is a great way to keep a block ready for on-the-go stitching, too!

6. Continuing to work one block at a time, refer to the appliqué placement diagram that appears with each pattern to position and appliqué the leaves and stems, and then the flower appliqués to each block. Finish by appliquéing the top edge of the basket on each block.

7. Trim each block to 12½" x 12½", making sure to keep the appliqué centered in the block.

PIECING THE BLOCKS, CORNERSTONES, AND SASHING

1. Referring to "Folded Triangles" (page 12), use your preferred marker and a ruler to draw a line from corner to corner on the wrong side of each 2" tan square.

2. With right sides together, place a marked square on each corner of an appliquéd block, noting the direction of the drawn line. Sew on the diagonal line; press. Trim the excess fabric, leaving a ¼" seam allowance.

3. With right sides together, place a marked 2" tan square on each corner of a 4" dark green square. The 2" tan squares will fit exactly on the 4" green squares with no overlap. Sew, press, and trim. Make 20 cornerstones.

Make 20.

4. With right sides together, sew a 1"-wide dark green strip between two 2"-wide tan strips along their long edges to make a strip set as shown; press. Make 11 strip sets. Crosscut the strip sets into a total of 31 segments, each 12½".

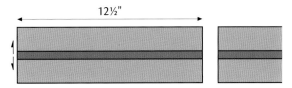

12½"

Make 11 strips sets.
Cut 31 segments.

ASSEMBLING THE QUILT TOP

1. Referring to the quilt assembly diagram below, arrange the blocks, sashing strips, and cornerstones as shown.

2. Sew four cornerstones and three horizontal sashing strips together to make a row as shown; press. Make five rows.

Make 5 rows.

3. Sew three blocks and four vertical sashing strips together to make a row as shown; press. Make four rows.

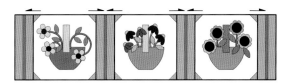

Make 4 rows.

4. Sew the rows from steps 2 and 3 together, alternating them as shown in the assembly diagram. Press the seams toward the sashing rows.

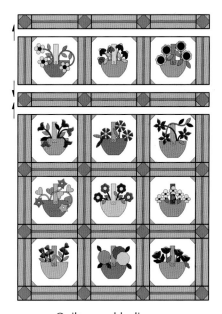

Quilt assembly diagram

5. Referring to "Adding the Borders" (page 12), use the 2" x 42" cream strips to make the side, top, and bottom inner borders for the quilt. Pin and sew the borders to the quilt. Press the seams toward the border.

6. Repeat step 5 using the 1½" x 42" dark green strips for the middle border, and the 6" x 42" red floral strips for the outer border. In each case, press the seams toward the newly added border.

FINISHING THE QUILT

Refer to "Finishing Techniques" (page 13) as needed to complete the following steps.

1. Layer, baste, and quilt your quilt. The quilt on page 22 was machine quilted by stitching in the ditch around the appliqué pieces, and close stippling was added in the block backgrounds and the cream inner border. The sashing was quilted with a pumpkin seed motif, and quilted feather designs finish off the outer border.

2. Bind the quilt using the 2½" x 42" red floral strips.

3. Sew a button to each basket handle as indicated on the appliqué pattern.

Quilt plan

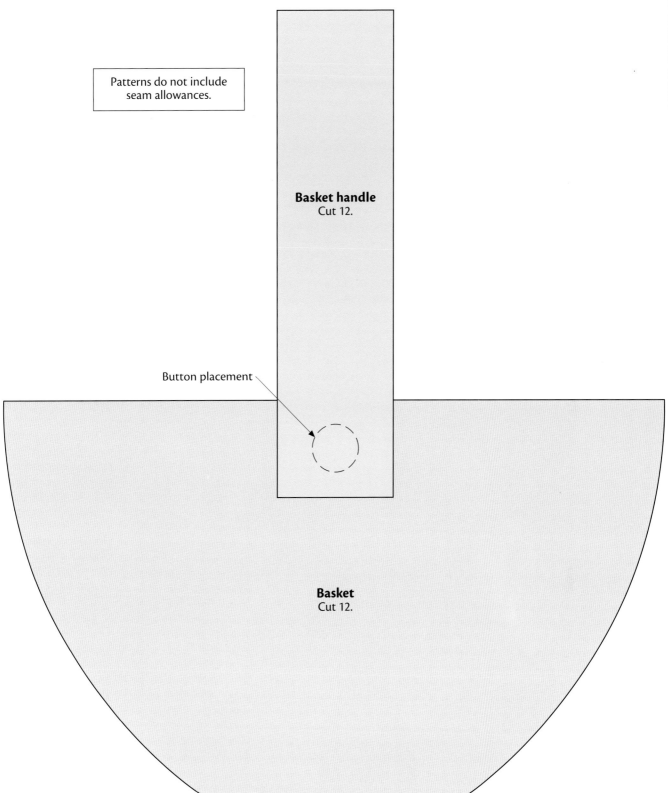

Patterns do not include
seam allowances.

Basket handle
Cut 12.

Button placement

Basket
Cut 12.

Patterns do not include
seam allowances.

Block 1

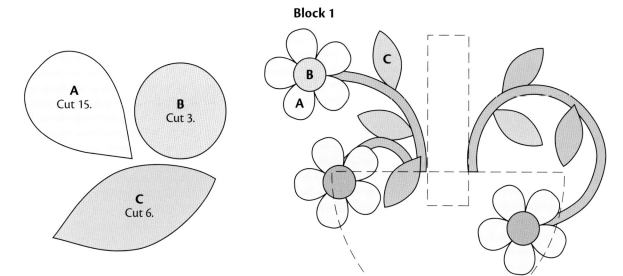

A
Cut 15.

B
Cut 3.

C
Cut 6.

Placement diagram

Block 2

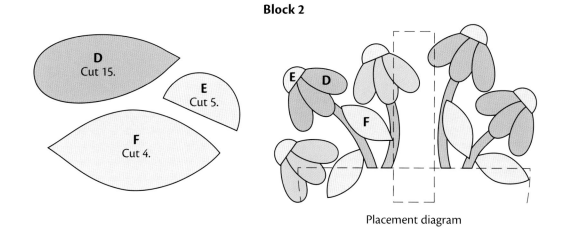

D
Cut 15.

E
Cut 5.

F
Cut 4.

Placement diagram

Block 3

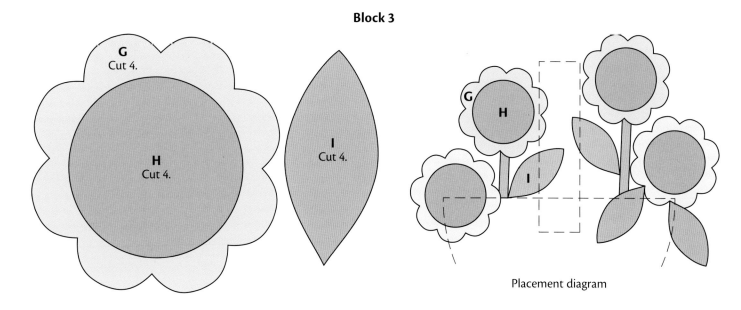

G
Cut 4.

H
Cut 4.

I
Cut 4.

Placement diagram

Patterns do not include
seam allowances.

Block 4

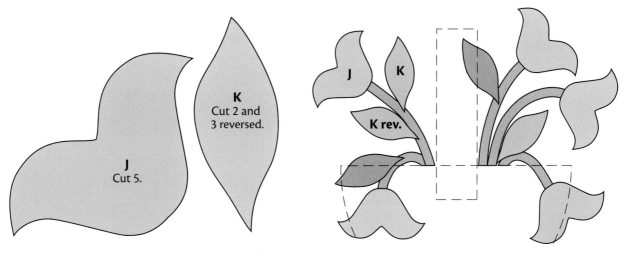

J
Cut 5.

K
Cut 2 and
3 reversed.

Placement diagram

Block 5

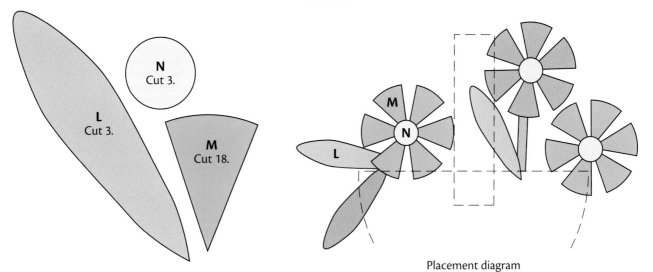

L
Cut 3.

N
Cut 3.

M
Cut 18.

Placement diagram

Block 6

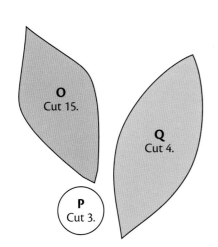

O
Cut 15.

Q
Cut 4.

P
Cut 3.

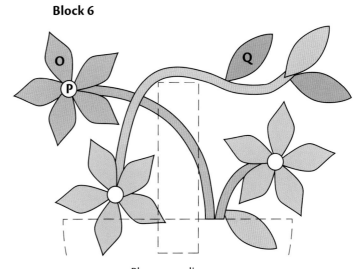

Placement diagram

Patterns do not include
seam allowances.

Block 7

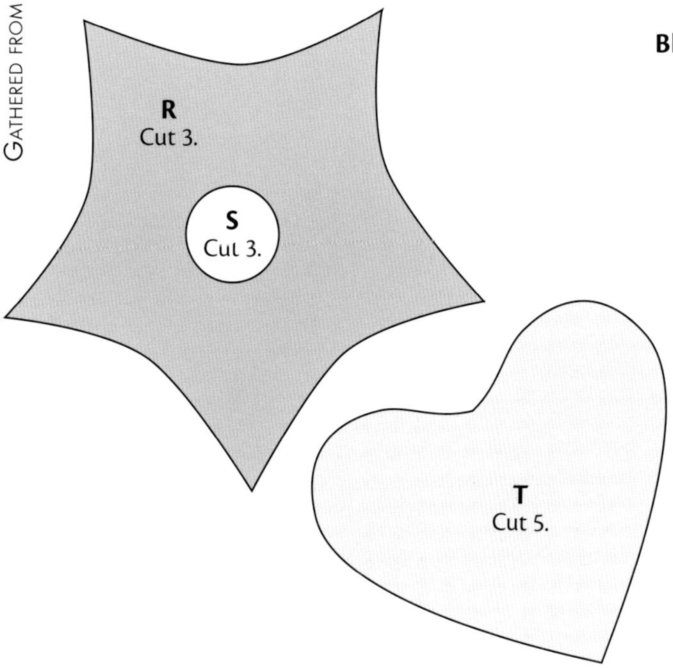

R
Cut 3.

S
Cut 3.

T
Cut 5.

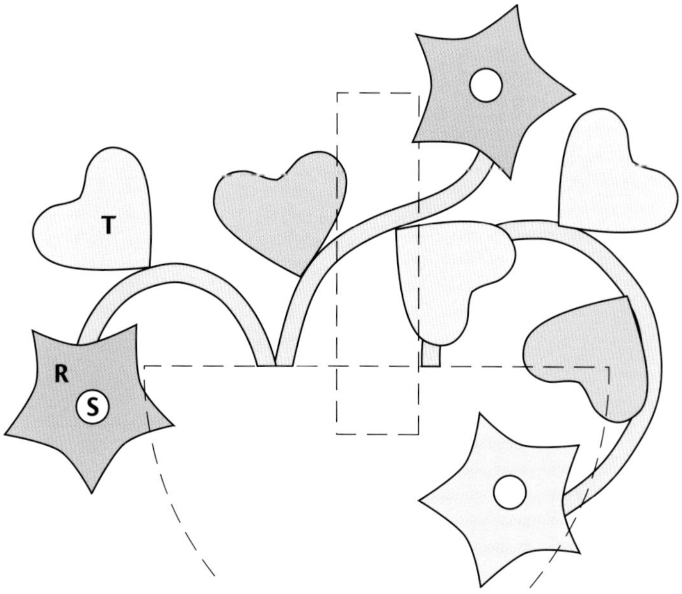

T

R
S

Placement diagram

Block 8

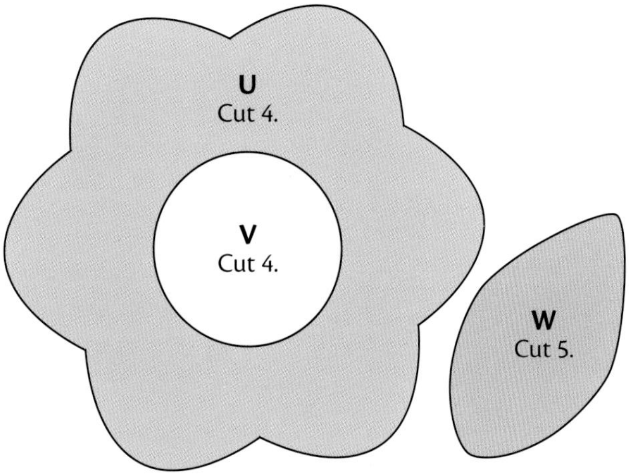

U
Cut 4.

V
Cut 4.

W
Cut 5.

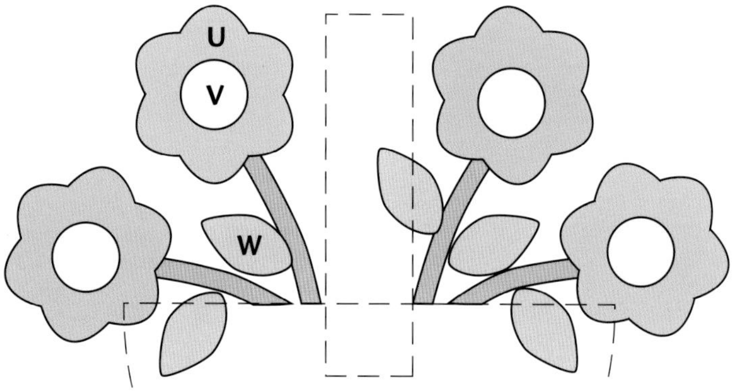

U
V

W

Placement diagram

Block 9

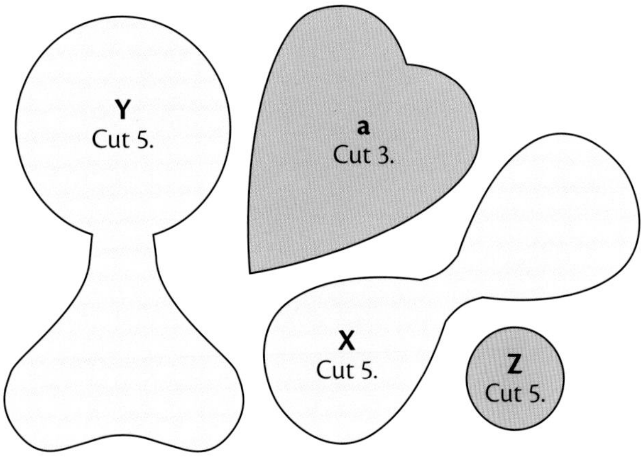

Y
Cut 5.

a
Cut 3.

X
Cut 5.

Z
Cut 5.

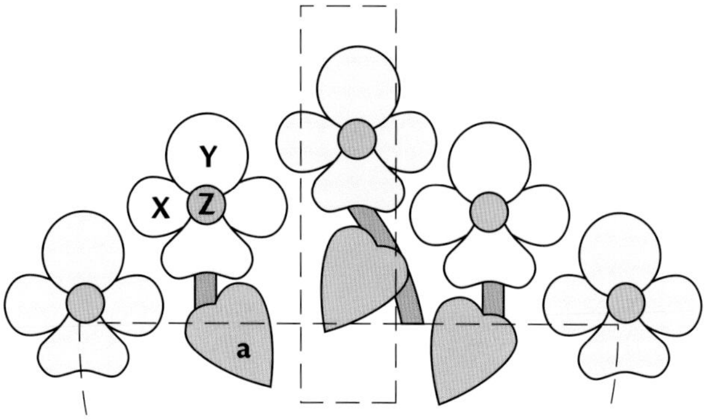

Y
X **Z**

a

Placement diagram

Patterns do not include
seam allowances.

Block 10

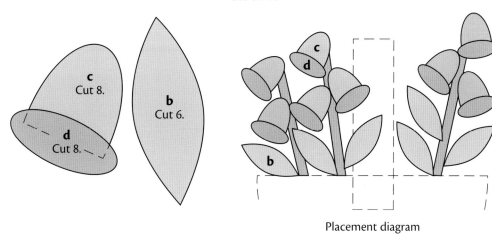

Placement diagram

Block 11

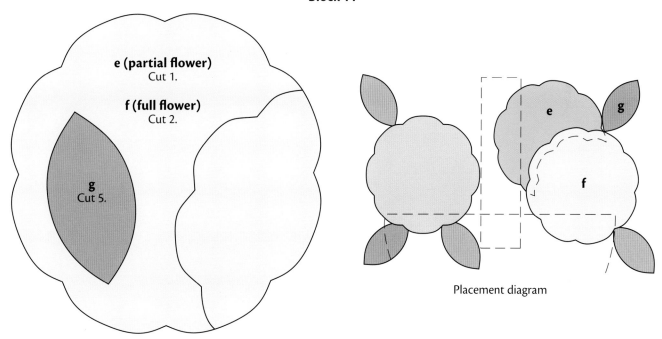

Placement diagram

Block 12

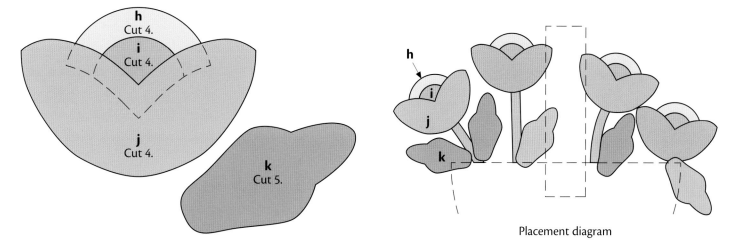

Placement diagram

Pieced, appliquéd, and quilted by Cindy Lammon.

Finished Wall Hanging: 37½" x 37½" • Finished Block: 12" x 12"

Gathered from the Garden Wall Hanging

MAKE FOUR OF YOUR FAVORITE FLOWER BASKET BLOCKS FROM "GATHERED FROM THE GARDEN" (PAGE 23) IN BRIGHT, CHEERY COLORS TO PERK UP ANY WALL!

MATERIALS

All yardages are based on 42"-wide fabric.

1⅔ yards of white tone-on-tone print for background, sashing, cornerstones, and border

⅞ yard of black-and-white checked fabric for basket appliqués and bias binding*

⅜ yard of green tone-on-tone print for sashing and cornerstones

6" x 13" scrap of black-and-white print for basket handle appliqués

Assorted scraps of green, blue, pink, and yellow fabrics for stems, leaf, and flower appliqués

1⅓ yards of backing fabric

40" x 40" piece of batting

4 buttons, ½" to ⅝" in diameter

If you prefer straight-grain binding, you will need ⅜ yard of this fabric.

CUTTING

Cut all strips across the width of the fabric unless otherwise noted.

From the white tone-on-tone print, cut:
2 strips, 13" x 42"; crosscut into 4 squares, 13" x 13"
11 strips, 1½" x 42"
2 strips, 2½" x 33½"
2 strips, 2½" x 37½"

From the green tone-on-tone print, cut:
7 strips, 1½" x 42"

From the *bias* of the black-and-white checked fabric, cut:
Enough 2½"-wide strips to total 165"*
For straight-grain binding, cut 5 strips, 2½" x 42".

APPLIQUÉING THE BLOCKS

Refer to "Hand-Appliqué Techniques" (page 17) and "Appliquéing the Blocks" (page 24) as needed.

Choose four of your favorite block designs from "Gathered from the Garden" (page 23). Use the desired patterns and the black-and-white check, black-and-white print, and assorted green, blue, pink, and yellow scraps to prepare and appliqué a basket, a basket handle, stems, leaves, and flower appliqués to each 13" white block. The patterns you select will tell you how many to cut of each piece, and how to deal with any reversed pieces. Make four blocks. Trim each block to 12½" x 12½", making sure to keep the appliqué centered in the block.

PIECING THE SASHING AND CORNERSTONES

1. With right sides together, sew a 1½" x 42" green strip between two 1½" x 42" white strips along their long edges to make a strip set as shown; press. Make five strip sets. Crosscut the strip sets into 12 segments, each 12½", and 9 segments, each 1½".

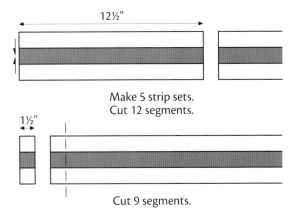

Make 5 strip sets.
Cut 12 segments.

Cut 9 segments.

2. With right sides together, sew a 1½" x 42" white strip between two 1½" x 42" green strips along their long edges to make a strip set as shown; press. Crosscut the strip set into 18 segments, each 1½".

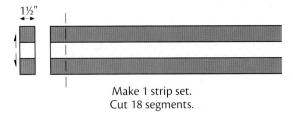

Make 1 strip set.
Cut 18 segments.

3. Sew one 1½" segment from step 1 between two segments from step 2 as shown; press. Make nine cornerstone units.

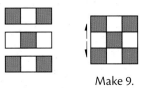

Make 9.

ASSEMBLING THE QUILT TOP

1. Referring to the quilt assembly diagram below, arrange the blocks, sashing strips, and cornerstones as shown.

2. Sew three cornerstones and two horizontal sashing strips together to make a row as shown in the assembly diagram; press. Make three rows.

3. Sew two blocks and three vertical sashing strips together to make a row as shown in the assembly diagram; press. Make two rows.

4. Sew the rows from steps 2 and 3 together, alternating them as shown in the assembly diagram. Press the seams toward the sashing rows.

Quilt assembly diagram

5. Referring to "Adding the Borders" (page 12), sew the 2½" x 33½" white strips to the sides of the quilt. Press the seams toward the border. Sew the 2½" x 37½" white strips to the top and bottom edges; press.

FINISHING THE WALL HANGING

Refer to "Finishing Techniques" (page 13) as needed to complete the following steps.

1. Layer, baste, and quilt your wall hanging. The wall hanging on page 32 was machine quilted by stitching in the ditch around the appliqués and closely stippling the backgrounds. The sashing was quilted in the ditch and the border was quilted with a scroll design.

2. Bind the quilt using the 2½"-wide black-and-white checked bias (or straight-grain) strips.

3. Sew a button to each basket handle as indicated on the appliqué pattern.

Quilt plan

Pieced, appliquéd, and quilted by Cindy Lammon.

Finished Quilt: 24½" x 24½" • Finished Block: 18" x 18"

Sunflower Circle

A SUNFLOWER IS SUCH A HAPPY FLOWER! APPLIQUÉ ONE FOR YOUR WALL AND IT WILL SURELY MAKE YOU SMILE.

MATERIALS

All yardages are based on 42"-wide fabric.

1⅛ yards of black tone-on-tone print for background, outer border, and binding

⅓ yard of green print for stem and leaf appliqués

¼ yard of yellow checked fabric for flower petal appliqués and inner border

6" x 6" scrap of rust print for flower center appliqué

⅞ yard of backing fabric

29" x 29" piece of batting

CUTTING

Cut all strips across the width of the fabric unless otherwise noted.

From the black tone-on-tone print, cut:
1 square, 19" x 19"
3 strips, 3" x 42"; crosscut into:
    2 strips, 3" x 19½"
    2 strips, 3" x 24½"
3 strips, 2½" x 42"

From the *bias* of the green print, cut:
8 strips, ⅞" x 3½"

From the yellow checked fabric, cut:
2 strips, 1" x 42"; crosscut into:
    2 strips, 1" x 18½"
    2 strips, 1" x 19½"

APPLIQUÉING THE BLOCK

Refer to "Hand-Appliqué Techniques" (page 17) for guidance as needed.

1. Fold the 19" black square in half in both directions and finger-crease to establish centering lines.

2. The pattern on page 39 represents one-fourth of the appliquéd sunflower design. Use a light box to align the creases in the background block with the long dashed lines on the quarter pattern, rotating the pattern around the center point to complete the design. Mark the center of the large sunflower circle (B) and single lines to identify the position of the stems.

(These marks will be covered by the appliqué pieces later.) If you wish, refer to "The Overlay Method" (page 18) and make an overlay of the sunflower to use when placing the petals.

3. Referring to "Stems" (page 19), use the ⅞" x 3½" green bias strips to prepare eight stems.

4. Use the pattern pieces on page 39 and the yellow checked fabric to prepare 12 sunflower petal appliqués (A), the rust scrap to prepare one sunflower center appliqué (B), and the remaining green print to prepare eight leaf appliqués (C). *You will need to reverse the asymmetrical leaf pattern when making your freezer-paper template in order for the leaf appliqués to face in the proper direction when they are sewn to the block.*

5. Refer to the photo on page 36 and the markings you made to position and appliqué the stems and then the sunflower petal, sunflower center, and leaf appliqués to the block background.

6. Trim the block to 18½" x 18½", making sure to keep the appliqué centered in the block.

ADDING BORDERS

1. Referring to the quilt assembly diagram below, sew the 1" x 18½" yellow strips to the sides of the block; press. Sew the 1" x 19½" yellow strips to the top and bottom edges; press.

2. Sew the 3" x 19½" black strips to the sides of the unit from step 1; press. Sew the 3" x 24½" black strips to the top and bottom; press.

Quilt assembly diagram

FINISHING THE QUILT

Refer to "Finishing Techniques" on page 13 as needed to complete the following steps.

1. Layer, baste, and quilt your quilt. A quilting design for the leaves is included on the leaf pattern (C) on page 39. In addition, the quilt on page 36 was machine quilted with stipple quilting in the background areas and with a meandering leaf design in the border.

2. Bind the quilt using the 2½" x 42" black strips.

Patterns do not include
seam allowances.

Rotate and align the pattern on the
dashed lines to complete the design.

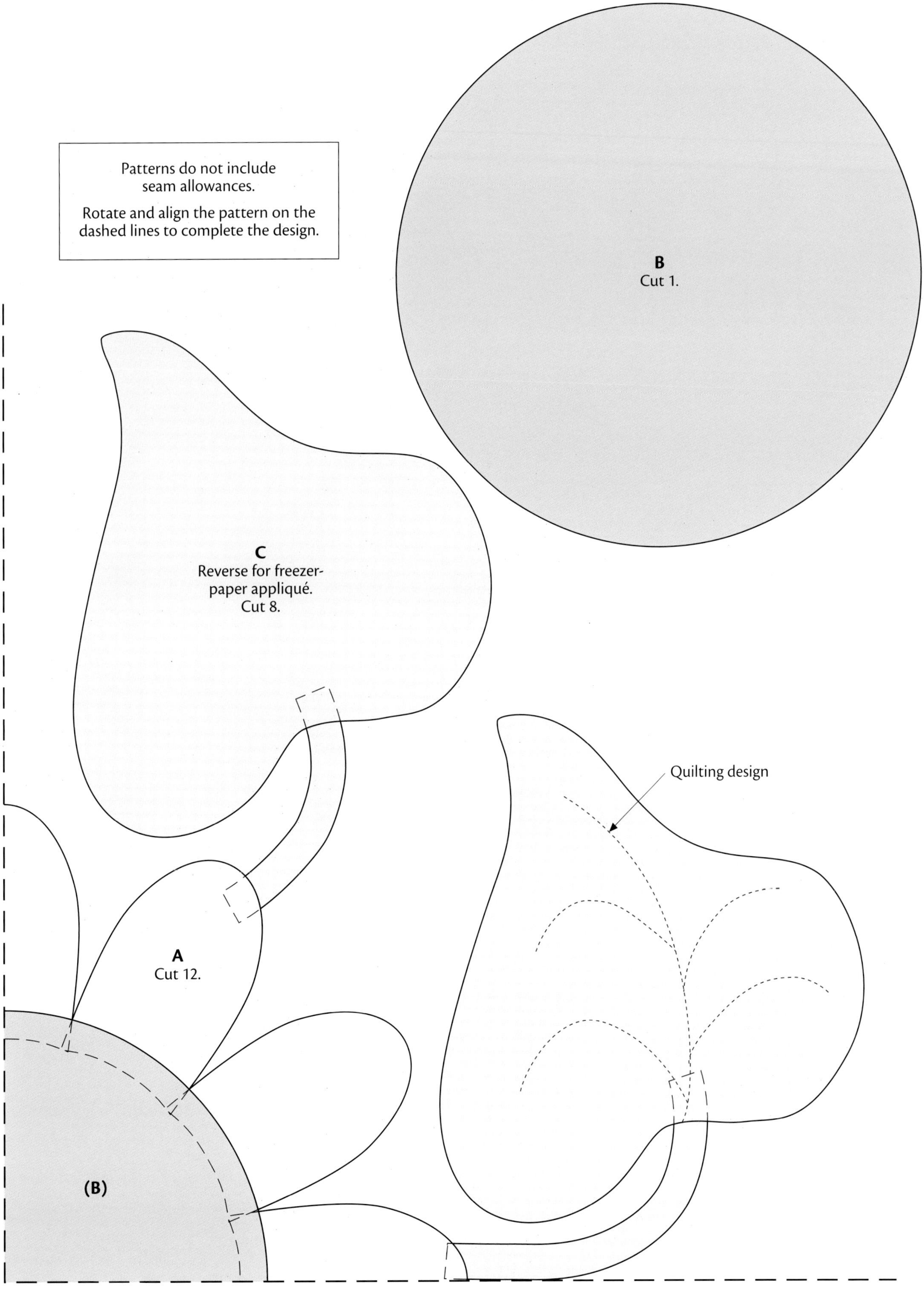

B
Cut 1.

C
Reverse for freezer-
paper appliqué.
Cut 8.

Quilting design

A
Cut 12.

(B)

Appliquéd, pieced, and quilted by Cindy Lammon.

Finished Quilt: 24½" x 24½" • Finished Block: 18" x 18"

Sunflower Circle with Pieced Border

ADDING A PIECED BORDER TO "SUNFLOWER CIRCLE" (PAGE 37) REALLY MAKES THE DESIGN SPARKLE!

MATERIALS

All yardages are based on 42"-wide fabric.

⅞ yard of cream tone-on-tone print for background and pieced border

⅔ yard of dark green print for stem and leaf appliqués, pieced border, and binding

⅜ yard of burgundy dotted print for flower center appliqué and pieced border

⅓ yard of gold print for flower petal appliqués and pieced border

⅞ yard of backing fabric

29" x 29" piece of batting

CUTTING

Cut all strips across the width of the fabric unless otherwise noted.

From the cream tone-on-tone print, cut:
1 square, 19" x 19"
1 strip, 4¼" x 20"; crosscut into 7 squares, 4¼" x 4¼". Cut each square twice diagonally to yield 28 quarter-square triangles.

From the dark green print, cut:
1 strip, 4¼" x 42"; crosscut into 6 squares, 4¼" x 4¼". Cut each square twice on the diagonal to yield 24 quarter-square triangles.
2 squares, 3⅞" x 3⅞"; cut each square once on the diagonal to yield 4 half-square triangles
3 strips, 2½" x 42"

From the *bias* of the remaining dark green print, cut:
8 strips, ⅞" x 3½"

From the burgundy dotted print, cut:

1 strip, 4¼" x 42"; crosscut into 6 squares, 4¼" x 4¼".
Cut each square twice on the diagonal to yield
24 quarter-square triangles.

From the gold print, cut:

1 strip, 4¼" x 42"; crosscut into 5 squares, 4¼" x 4¼".
Cut each square twice on the diagonal to yield
20 quarter-square triangles.

2 squares, 3⅞" x 3⅞"; cut each square once on the
diagonal to yield 4 half-square triangles

APPLIQUÉING THE BLOCK

Refer to "Hand-Appliqué Techniques" (page 17) and
"Appliquéing the Block" (page 37) as needed to
complete the following steps.

1. Use the pattern on page 39 to prepare the 19"
    cream block for appliqué.

2. Use the ⅞" x 3½" green bias strips to prepare
    eight stems. Use the pattern pieces on page
    39 and the gold print to prepare 12 sunflower
    petal appliqués (A), the burgundy print to
    prepare the sunflower center appliqué (B), and
    the remaining green print to prepare eight
    leaf appliqués (C). *You will need to reverse the
    asymmetrical leaf pattern when making your
    freezer-paper template in order for the leaf
    appliqués to face in the proper direction when
    they are sewn to the block.*

3. Refer to the photo on page 40 and the
    markings you made in step 1 to position and
    appliqué the stems, and then the sunflower
    petal, sunflower center, and leaf appliqués to
    the block background.

4. Trim the block to 18½" x 18½", making sure to
    keep the appliqué centered in the block.

PIECING AND ADDING THE BORDER

1. With right sides together, sew a cream quarter-
    square triangle and a gold quarter-square
    triangle together along their long diagonal
    edges as shown; press. Be very careful pressing
    these units so that the outer, bias edges don't
    get stretched! Make 20.

Make 20.

2. With right sides together, sew a burgundy
    quarter-square triangle to the adjacent gold
    sides of a unit from step 1 as shown; press. Make
    four and label them unit A.

Unit A.
Make 4.

3. With right sides together, sew a green quarter-
    square triangle and a burgundy quarter-square
    triangle to opposite sides of a unit from step 1,
    placing them carefully as shown; press. Make 16
    and label them unit B.

Unit B.
Make 16.

4. Sew one of unit A and four of unit B together
    to make a row as shown. Press these seams
    open to reduce bulk. Make four rows.

Make 4.

5. With right sides together, sew a cream quarter-square triangle to the short sides of a gold half-square triangle as shown. Press, again being mindful of the outside bias edges. Make four.

Make 4.

6. With right sides together, sew a green quarter-square triangle to opposite ends of a unit from step 5 as shown; press. Sew a green half-square triangle to the top of the unit; press. Make four and label them unit C.

Unit C.
Make 4.

7. Referring to the quilt assembly diagram below, sew a border unit from step 4 to each side of the Sunflower block. Press the seams toward the block. Sew a unit C to each corner of the quilt. Press the seams toward unit C.

Quilt assembly diagram

FINISHING THE QUILT

Refer to "Finishing Techniques" on page 13 as needed to complete the following steps.

1. Layer, baste, and quilt your quilt. A quilting design for the leaves is included on the leaf pattern (C) on page 39. In addition, the quilt on page 40 was machine quilted with stipple quilting and quarter sunflower motifs in the background areas. The pieced border was quilted in the ditch.

2. Bind the quilt using the 2½" x 42" green strips.

Garden Wreath Table Runner

BRING YOUR GARDEN FLOWERS TO THE TABLE BY APPLIQUÉING A WREATH OR TWO ON THIS SIMPLE TABLE RUNNER. THE CENTER BLOCK IS LEFT PLAIN FOR DISPLAYING A VASE OF REAL FLOWERS!

Pieced, appliquéd, and quilted by Cindy Lammon.

Finished Table Runner: 17½" x 51½" • Finished Block: 12" x 12"

MATERIALS

All yardages are based on 42"-wide fabric.

⅔ yard of white tone-on-tone print for background and setting triangles

⅝ yard of coordinating multicolored floral print for setting triangles

½ yard of green dotted print for appliqué blocks and setting triangles

⅛ yard *each* of 2 different green prints for stems and leaf appliqués

Assorted scraps of blue and yellow prints for flower appliqués

⅝ yard of green striped fabric for bias binding*

1⅝ yards of backing fabric

22" x 56" piece of batting

*If you prefer straight-grain binding, you will need ⅜ yard of this fabric.

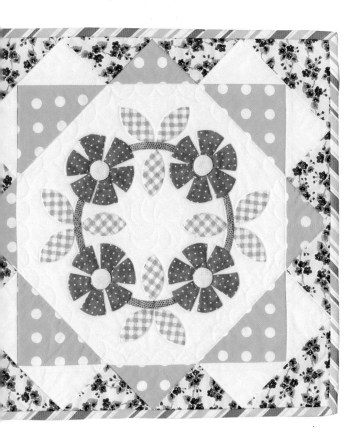

CUTTING

Cut all strips across the width of the fabric unless otherwise noted. Many of the triangles are close in size; I suggest separating them into labeled, resealable plastic bags as you cut to keep the pieces organized.

From the white tone-on-tone print, cut:
2 squares, 13" x 13"
1 square, 12½" x 12½"
2 strips, 3⅞" x 42"; crosscut into 12 squares, 3⅞" x 3⅞".
　　Cut each square once on the diagonal to yield a total of 24 half-square A triangles.

From the *bias* of one of the 2 different green prints, cut:
8 strips, ⅞" x 3½"

From the green dotted print, cut:
2 strips, 3½" x 42"; crosscut into 12 squares, 3½" x 3½"
1 strip, 7¼" x 42"; crosscut into 3 squares, 7¼" x 7¼".
　　Cut each square twice on the diagonal to yield 12 quarter-square B triangles.

From the coordinating multicolored floral print, cut:
1 strip, 5½" x 42"; crosscut into 4 squares, 5½" x 5½".
　　Cut each square twice on the diagonal to yield 16 quarter-square C triangles.
1 square, 9¾" x 9¾"; cut twice on the diagonal to yield 4 quarter-square D triangles
4 squares, 3½" x 3½"
2 squares, 5⅛" x 5⅛"; cut each square once on the diagonal to yield 4 E half-square triangles

From the *bias* of the green striped fabric, cut:
Enough 2½"-wide strips to total 148" *

*For straight-grain binding, cut 4 strips, 2½" x 42".

APPLIQUÉING THE BLOCKS

Refer to "Hand-Appliqué Techniques" (page 17) for guidance as needed.

1.　Fold each 13" white square in half in both directions and finger-crease to establish centering lines.

2. The pattern on page 49 represents one-fourth of the appliquéd wreath design. Align the creases in the background block with the long dashed lines on the quarter pattern, rotating the pattern around the center point to complete the design. Mark single lines to identify the position of the stems and tiny guide marks for placing the leaves. (These marks will be covered by the appliqué pieces later.) If you wish, refer to "The Overlay Method" (page 18) and make an overlay of the flower to use when placing the petals.

3. Referring to "Stems" (page 19), use the ⅞" x 3½" green bias strips to prepare stems.

4. Use the pattern pieces on page 49 and the assorted blue scraps to prepare 48 petal appliqués (A), the assorted yellow scraps to prepare eight flower center appliqués (B), and the second green print to prepare 24 leaf appliqués (C). There are no reverse pattern pieces in this design.

5. Refer to the photo on pages 44–45 and the markings you made to position and appliqué the four stems, and then 24 petal, four flower center, and 12 leaf appliqués to each block background.

6. Trim the blocks to 12½" x 12½", making sure to keep the appliqué centered in the block.

7. Referring to "Folded Triangles" (page 12), use your preferred marker and a ruler to draw a line from corner to corner on the wrong side of each 3½" green dotted square.

8. With right sides together, place a marked square on each corner of an appliquéd block, noting the direction of the drawn line. Sew on the diagonal line; press. Trim the excess fabric, leaving a ¼" seam allowance. Make two.

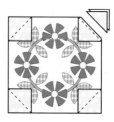 

9. Repeat step 8, substituting the 12½" white square for the appliquéd block.

PIECING THE SETTING TRIANGLES

1. With right sides together, sew a white half-square A triangle to the short sides of a green dotted quarter-square B triangle as shown; press. Make 12.

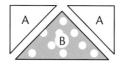 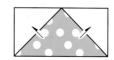

Make 12.

2. With right sides together, sew a floral C quarter-square triangle to the right short edge of a unit from step 1 as shown; press. Make four.

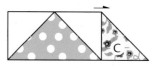

Make 4.

3. With right sides together, sew a floral quarter-square C triangle to the left short edge of a unit from step 1 as shown; press. Make four.

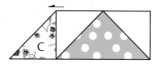

Make 4.

4. Sew a floral quarter-square D triangle to a unit from step 2 as shown; press. Make four.

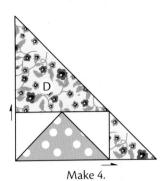

Make 4.

5. Sew a 3½" floral square to a unit from step 3 as shown; press. Make four.

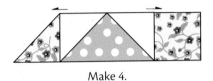

Make 4.

6. Sew a unit from steps 4 and 5 together to complete a side setting triangle as shown; press. Make four.

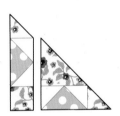 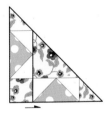

Make 4.

7. Sew a floral quarter-square C triangle to opposite ends of a remaining unit from step 1 as shown; press. Sew a floral half-square E triangle to the top of the unit to complete a corner setting triangle; press. Make four.

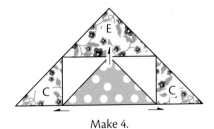

Make 4.

ASSEMBLING THE TABLE RUNNER

Referring to the table runner assembly diagram below, arrange the appliqué blocks, the plain block, the side setting triangles, and the corner setting triangles as shown. Sew the blocks and side setting triangles together in diagonal rows. Press the seams toward the setting triangles. Finish by adding the corner setting triangles; press.

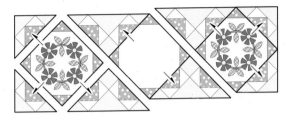

Table runner assembly diagram

FINISHING THE TABLE RUNNER

Refer to "Finishing Techniques" (page 13) as needed to complete the following steps.

1. Layer, baste, and quilt your table runner. The table runner on pages 44–45 was machine quilted with in-the-ditch stitching around the pieced shapes and additional lines in the large triangles. The appliqué blocks were quilted in the ditch around the appliqué shapes. A small floral motif was quilted in the center of each wreath, and each block was surrounded by a small scalloped design. The plain block was quilted with a large feathered motif.

2. Bind the quilt using the 2½"-wide striped bias (or straight-grain) strips.

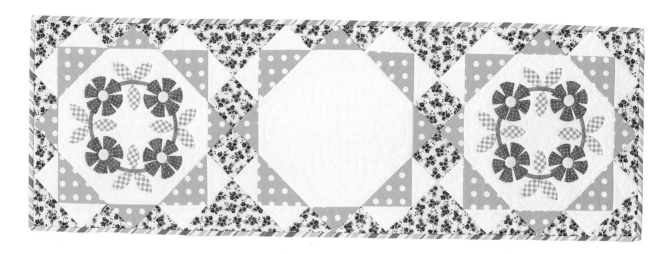

SEASONAL FLOWER OPTIONS

You can make a variety of seasonal table runners simply by changing the flowers on the appliquéd wreaths in the original design (top photo). Try any of the 12" tulip blocks from "Tiptoe through the Tulips" (page 51); additional patterns are given on page 49 for a poinsettia (bottom photo), a sunflower, and a rose.

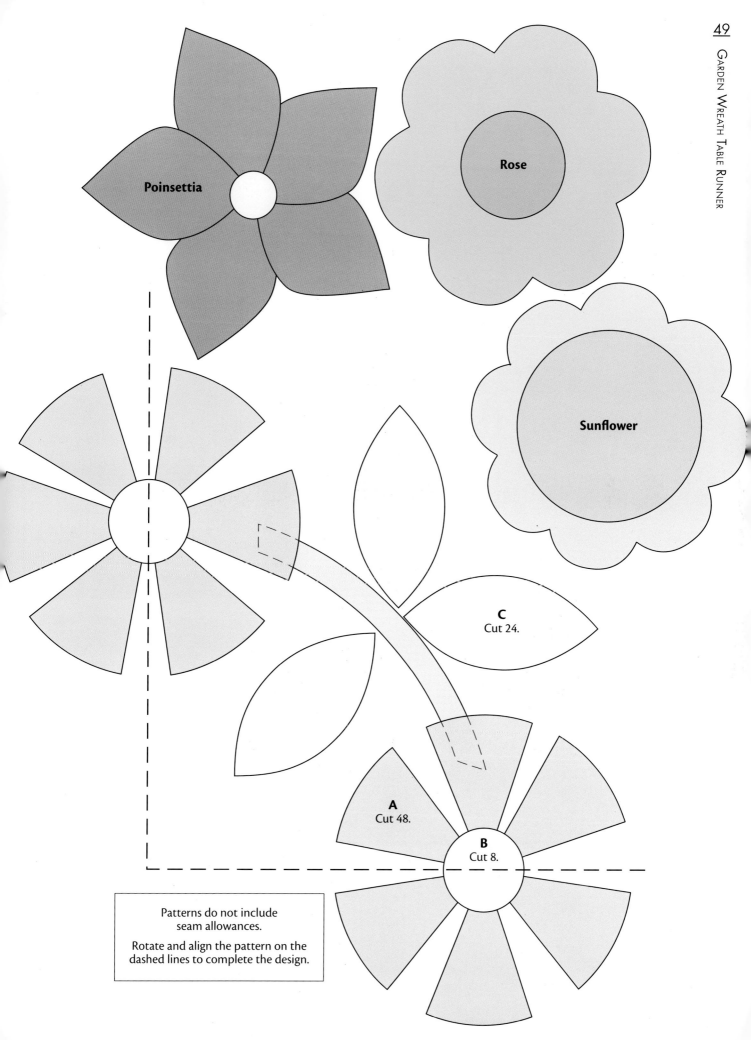

Poinsettia

Rose

Sunflower

C
Cut 24.

A
Cut 48.

B
Cut 8.

Patterns do not include
seam allowances.

Rotate and align the pattern on the
dashed lines to complete the design.

Appliquéd, pieced, and quilted by Cindy Lammon.

Finished Quilt: 52½" x 52½" • Finished Block: 12" x 12"

Tiptoe through the Tulips

TULIPS POPPING OUT OF THE GROUND ARE A SURE SIGN OF SPRING! CHASE AWAY THE WINTER BLUES WITH THESE CHEERY RED TULIPS, ALL MADE FROM FABRIC.

MATERIALS

All yardages are based on 42"-wide fabric.

2 yards of tone-on-tone cream print for backgrounds, sawtooth border, and outer border

1½ yards *total* of assorted red prints for flower appliqués and sawtooth border

1½ yards of dark green print for sashing and binding

Assorted scraps of green prints for stems and leaf appliqués

5" x 8" scrap of black print for vase

3¼ yards of backing fabric

57" x 57" piece of batting

CUTTING

Cut all fabrics across the width of the fabric unless otherwise noted.

From the cream tone-on-tone print, cut:

3 strips, 13" x 42"; crosscut into 9 squares, 13" x 13"

4 strips, 2⅞" x 42"; crosscut into 44 squares, 2⅞" x 2⅞". Cut each square once on the diagonal to make 88 half-square triangles.

4 squares, 2½" x 2½"

6 strips, 2½" x 42"

From the assorted scraps of green prints, cut:

Enough ⅞"-wide strips to total approximately 45"

From the *bias* of the assorted scraps of green prints, cut:

Enough ⅞"-wide strips to total approximately 95"

From the *lengthwise grain* of the dark green print, cut:

8 strips, 2½" x the fabric length; crosscut into:

  4 strips, 2½" x 44½"

  12 strips, 2½" x 12½"

5 strips, 2½" x the fabric length

From the assorted red prints, cut *a total of*:

44 squares, 2⅞" x 2⅞"; cut each square once on the diagonal to make 88 half-square triangles

Block 1

Block 2

Block 3

Block 4

Block 5

Block 6

Block 7

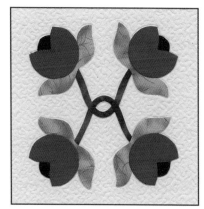

Block 8

Block 9

APPLIQUÉING THE BLOCKS

Refer to "Hand-Appliqué Techniques" (page 17) for guidance as needed.

1. Fold each 13" cream square in half in both directions and finger-crease to establish centering lines.

2. The patterns on pages 55–63 represent one-fourth or one-half of each appliqué design. Align the creases on each background block with the long dashed lines on the partial pattern, rotating or flipping the pattern to complete the design. Mark single lines to identify the position of the stems and tiny guide marks for placing the leaves. (These marks will be covered by the appliqué pieces later.) If you wish, refer to "The Overlay Method" (page 18) and make overlays of the tulips for placing the various tulip pieces.

3. Referring to "Stems" (page 19), use the ⅞"-wide assorted green strips to prepare the required length of straight-grain and bias stems as described in the cutting list. As you make the blocks, you will cut curved stems from the prepared bias strips and straight stems from the prepared straight-grain strips.

4. Working one block at a time, use the pattern pieces on pages 55–63 and the remaining assorted red prints to prepare the tulip appliqués (petals and flower centers) for each block. From the remaining assorted green prints, prepare the leaf appliqués for each block. The patterns tell you how many to cut of each piece, and how to deal with any reversed pieces. Refer to the photos opposite for color guidance as needed. The tip box "Stay Organized" (page 24) includes an idea for keeping the multiple pieces in order.

5. Refer to the photos and the markings you made in step 2 to position and appliqué the stems and then the tulip and leaf appliqués to each block. See "Exceptions to the Rule" below for a few minor exceptions.

6. Trim each block to 12½" x 12½", making sure to keep the appliqué centered in the block.

EXCEPTIONS TO THE RULE

Anyone who has been quilting a while knows that there is no rule that can't be broken—or at least bent! In all the patterns in this book so far, stems usually have been appliquéd before any leaves or flowers are stitched to the block. Three blocks in this quilt vary from this pattern:

-   Block 4: Appliqué L pieces first, then the stems, and then the remaining pieces.
-   Block 7: Appliqué U pieces, then the stems, and then the remaining pieces.
-   Block 9: Appliqué piece d, then the stems, and then the remaining pieces.

ASSEMBLING THE QUILT

1. Referring to the quilt assembly diagram on page 54, arrange the blocks, the 2½" x 12½" green vertical sashing strips, and the 2½" x 44½" green horizontal sashing strips as shown.

2. Sew three blocks and four vertical sashing strips together to make a row as shown in the assembly diagram; press. Make three rows.

3. Sew the rows from step 2 and the horizontal sashing strips together, alternating them as shown in the assembly diagram; press.

Quilt assembly diagram

4. With right sides together, sew an assorted red half-square triangle and a cream half-square triangle together along their long diagonal edges as shown. Make 88.

Make 88.

5. Sew 22 units from step 4 in a row, turning the triangles as shown; press. Make four rows.

Make 4.

6. Referring to the quilt plan at right, sew a row from step 5 to the top and bottom of the quilt. Press the seams toward the quilt center. Sew a 2½" cream square to each end of each remaining row. Press the seams toward the squares. Sew these rows to the sides; press.

7. Referring to "Adding the Borders" (page 12), use the 2½"-wide cream strips to make the side, top, and bottom outer borders for the quilt. Pin and sew the borders to the quilt. Press the seams toward the border.

FINISHING THE QUILT

Refer to "Finishing Techniques" (page 13) as needed to complete the following steps.

1. Layer, baste, and quilt your quilt. The quilt on page 50 was machine quilted by stitching in the ditch around the appliqué pieces, and with close stippling in the block backgrounds. The sashing was quilted with straight lines, the triangles in the sawtooth border were stitched in the ditch, and the outer cream border was quilted with a half-feather design.

2. Bind the quilt using the 2½" x 42" green strips.

Quilt plan

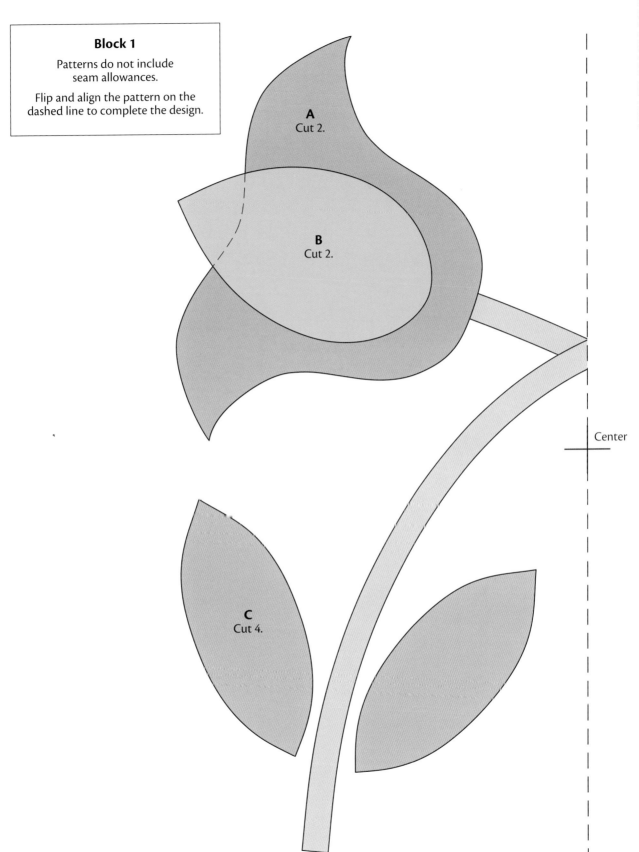

Block 1

Patterns do not include
seam allowances.

Flip and align the pattern on the
dashed line to complete the design.

A
Cut 2.

B
Cut 2.

C
Cut 4.

Center

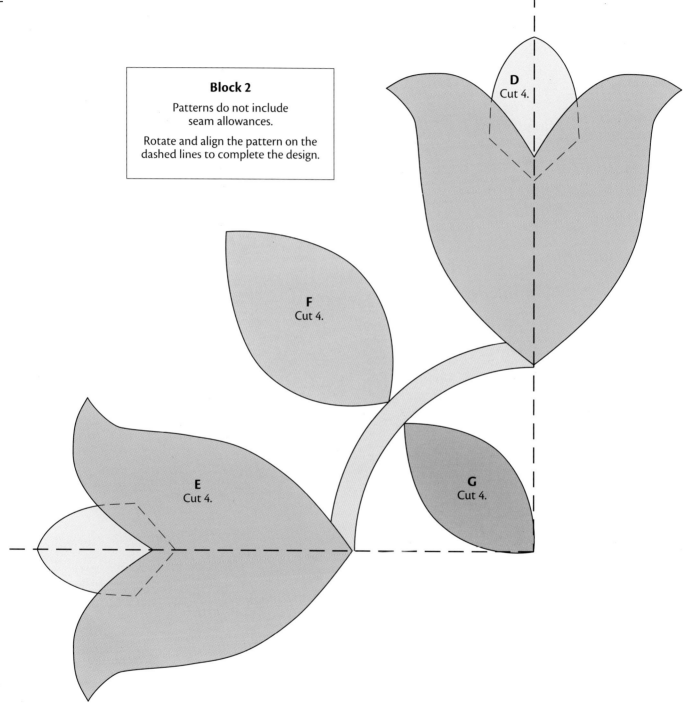

Block 2

Patterns do not include
seam allowances.

Rotate and align the pattern on the
dashed lines to complete the design.

D
Cut 4.

F
Cut 4.

E
Cut 4.

G
Cut 4.

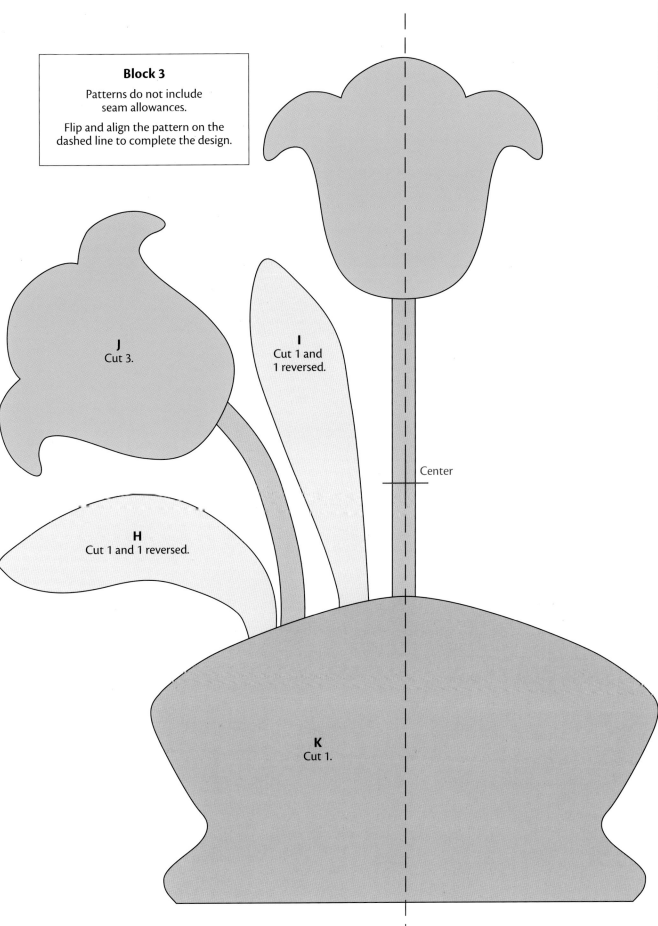

Block 3

Patterns do not include seam allowances.

Flip and align the pattern on the dashed line to complete the design.

J
Cut 3.

I
Cut 1 and
1 reversed.

H
Cut 1 and 1 reversed.

Center

K
Cut 1.

Block 4

Patterns do not include
seam allowances.

Rotate and align the pattern on the
dashed lines to complete the design.

M
Cut 4.

L
Cut 4.
Reverse for
freezer-paper
appliqué.

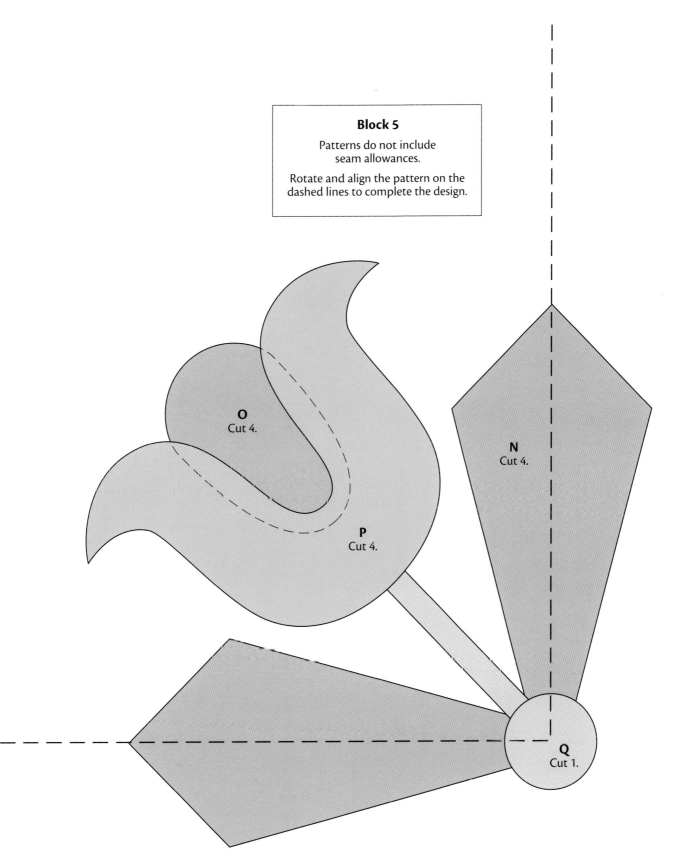

Block 5

Patterns do not include
seam allowances.

Rotate and align the pattern on the
dashed lines to complete the design.

O
Cut 4.

P
Cut 4.

N
Cut 4.

Q
Cut 1.

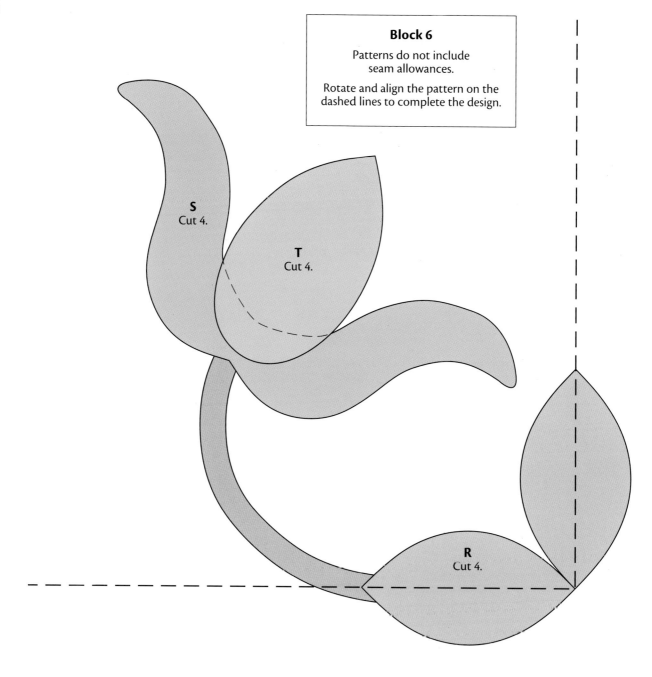

Block 6

Patterns do not include
seam allowances.

Rotate and align the pattern on the
dashed lines to complete the design.

S
Cut 4.

T
Cut 4.

R
Cut 4.

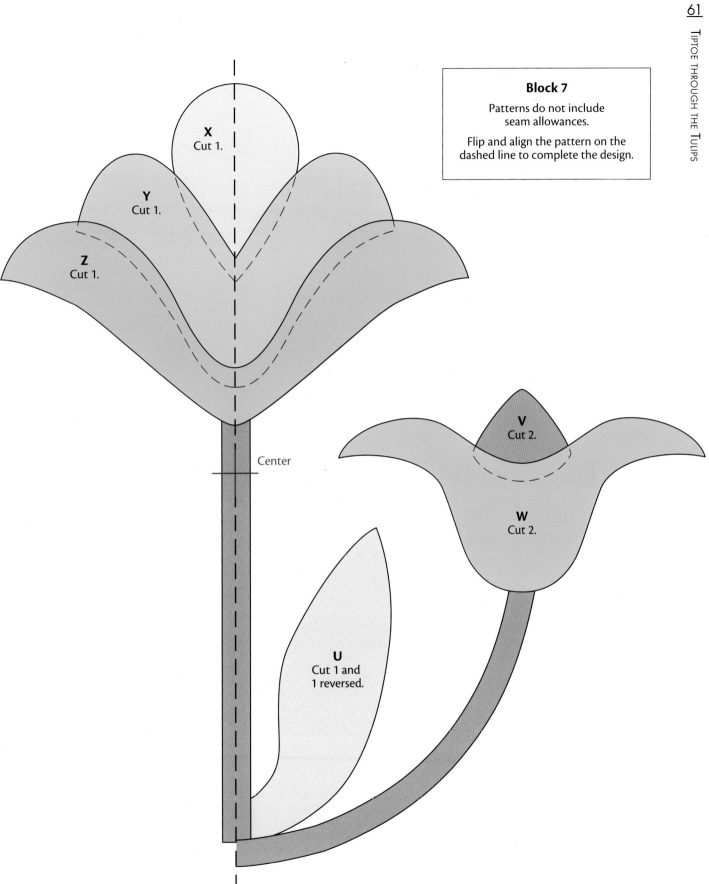

Block 7

Patterns do not include
seam allowances.

Flip and align the pattern on the
dashed line to complete the design.

X
Cut 1.

Y
Cut 1.

Z
Cut 1.

Center

V
Cut 2.

W
Cut 2.

U
Cut 1 and
1 reversed.

Block 8

Patterns do not include
seam allowances.

Rotate and align the pattern on the
dashed lines to complete the design.

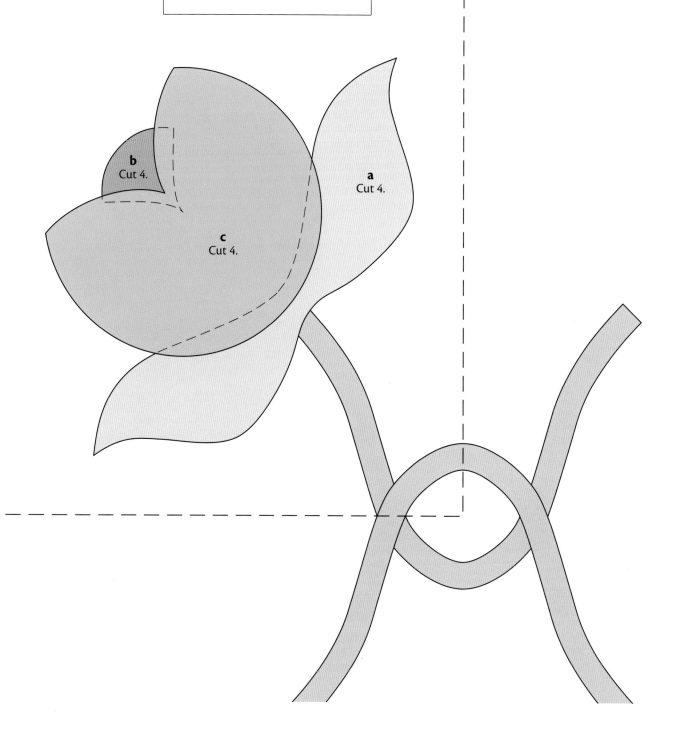

b
Cut 4.

a
Cut 4.

c
Cut 4.

e
Cut 1.

Block 9

Patterns do not include
seam allowances.

Flip and align the pattern on the
dashed line to complete the design.

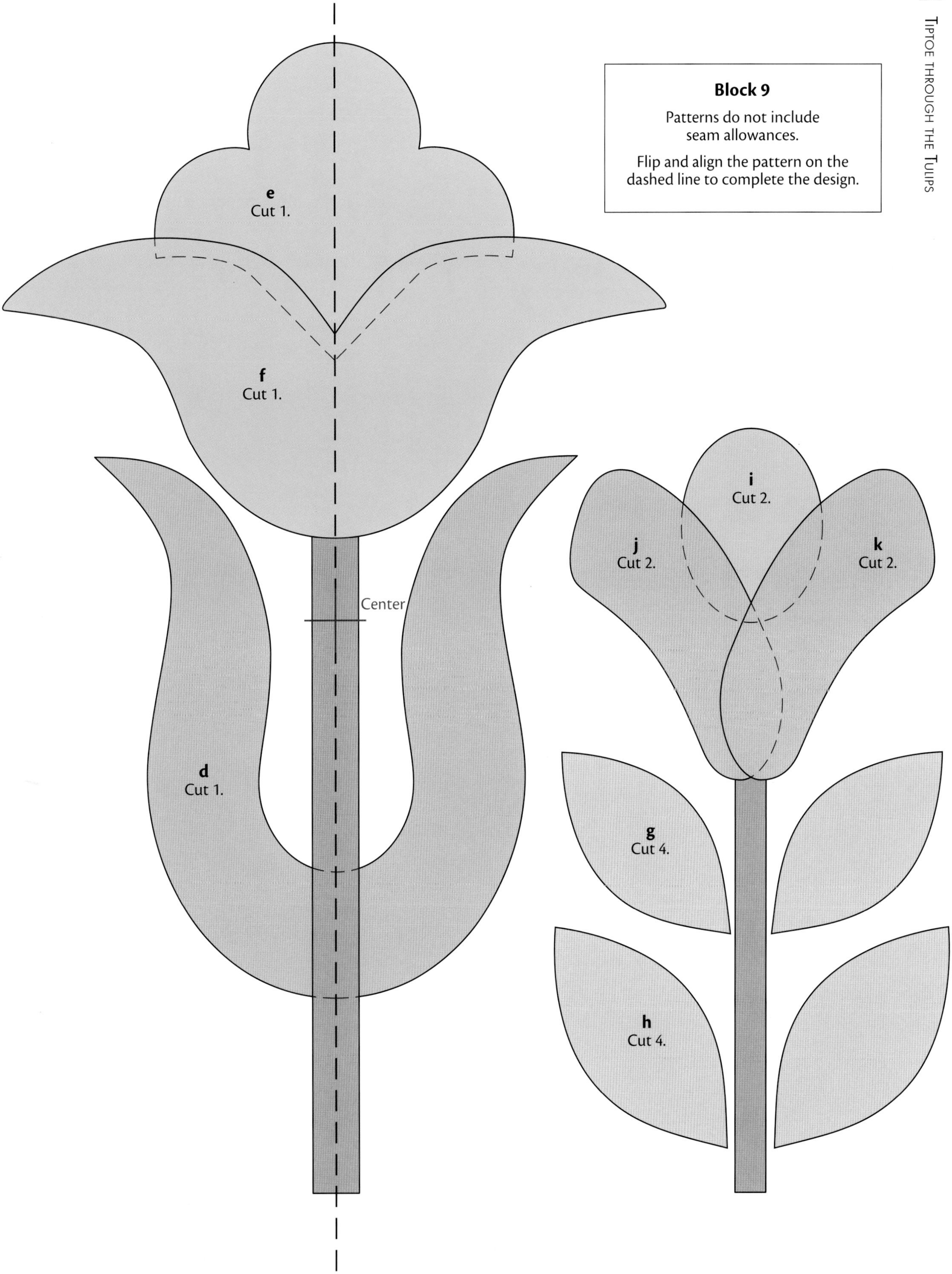

f
Cut 1.

i
Cut 2.

j
Cut 2.

k
Cut 2.

Center

d
Cut 1.

g
Cut 4.

h
Cut 4.

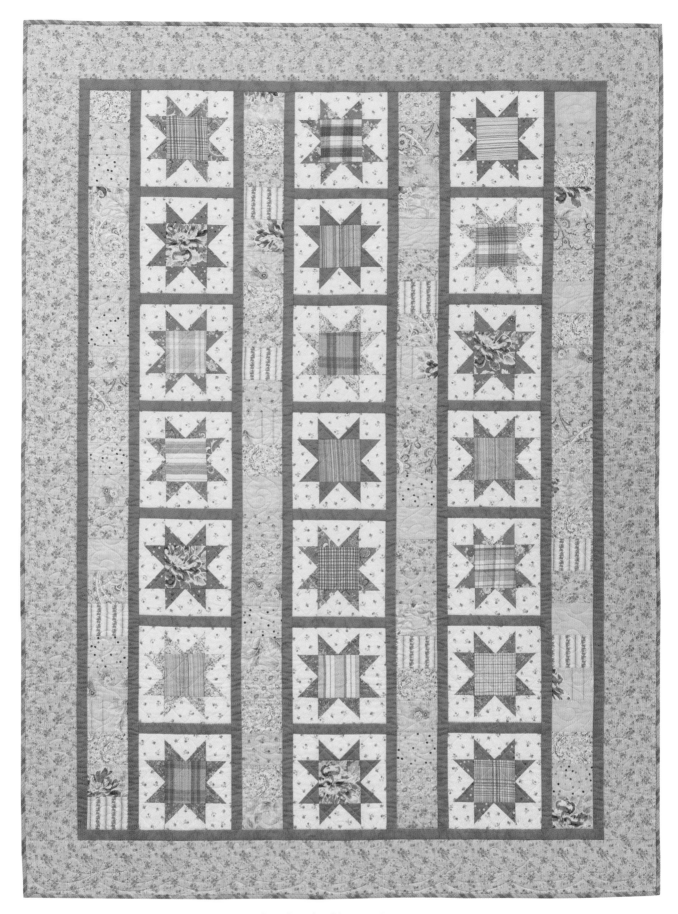

Pieced and quilted by Cindy Lammon.

Finished Quilt: 61½" x 81½" • Finished Block: 9" x 9"

Down the Garden Path

THE COMBINATION OF LARGE AND SMALL FLORAL PRINTS, PLAIDS, STRIPES, AND PAISLEYS CREATES THE SOFT, RELAXING LOOK OF A COTTAGE GARDEN IN THIS QUILT.

MATERIALS

All yardages are based on 42"-wide fabric.

1⅔ yards of yellow print for block backgrounds

1⅓ yards *total* of assorted green prints for pieced sashing

1¼ yards of pink tone-on-tone print for sashing

1¼ yards of green floral print for outer border

1 yard *total* of assorted pink prints for star points

4½" x 4½" squares of 21 assorted pink-and-green prints and plaids for star centers

⅞ yard of pink-and-green plaid for bias binding*

4⅞ yards of fabric for backing

66" x 85" piece of batting

If you prefer straight-grain binding, you will need ⅔ yard of this fabric.

CUTTING

Cut all strips across the width of the fabric unless otherwise noted.

From the assorted pink prints, cut *a total of:*
168 squares, 2½" x 2½", in matching sets of 8

From the yellow print, cut:
11 strips, 3" x 42"; crosscut into 84 rectangles, 3" x 4½"
7 strips, 3" x 42"; crosscut into 84 squares, 3" x 3"

From the assorted green prints, cut *a total of:*
92 rectangles, 3½" x 4½"

From the pink tone-on-tone print, cut:
25 strips, 1½" x 42"; crosscut 5 strips into 18 rectangles, 1½" x 9½"

From the green floral print, cut:
7 strips, 5½" x 42"

From the *bias* of the pink-and-green plaid, cut:
Enough 2½"-wide strips to total 300" *

For straight-grain binding, cut 8 strips, 2½" x 42".

MAKING THE BLOCKS

1. Referring to "Folded Triangles" on page 12, use your preferred marker and a ruler to draw a line from corner to corner on the wrong side of each 2½" assorted pink square.

2. With right sides together, place one marked square on the corner of a 3" x 4½" yellow rectangle as shown, noting the direction of the drawn line. Sew on the diagonal line; press. Trim the excess fabric, leaving a ¼" seam allowance. Repeat to sew a matching 2½" pink square to the yellow rectangle as shown; press and trim. Make 84 units in matching sets of four.

Make 84 in
matching sets of 4.

3. Arrange four matching units from step 2, four 3" yellow squares, and a 4½" assorted plaid or print square as shown. Sew the units and squares together into rows; press. Sew the rows together; press. Make 21 blocks.

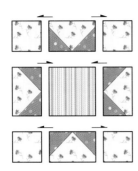 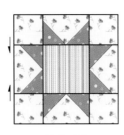

Make 21.

MAKING THE PIECED SASHING

Sew twenty-three 3½" x 4½" assorted green rectangles together along their long edges to make a row as shown; press. Make four rows.

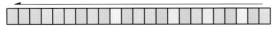

Make 4.

ASSEMBLING THE QUILT TOP

1. Arrange seven Star blocks and six 1½" x 9½" pink tone-on-tone rectangles, alternating them as shown. Sew the blocks and rectangles together into rows; press. Make three rows.

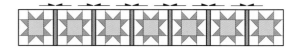

2. Sew two remaining 1½" pink tone-on-tone strips together end to end; press. Make 10. Trim eight strips to measure 1½" x 69½", and two strips to measure 1½" x 51½".

3. Referring to the quilt assembly diagram below, arrange and sew the rows from step 1, the 1½" x 69½" pink tone-on-tone strips from step 2, and the pieced sashing strips together as shown; press. Sew the 1½" x 51½" pink tone-on-tone strips from step 2 to the top and bottom; press.

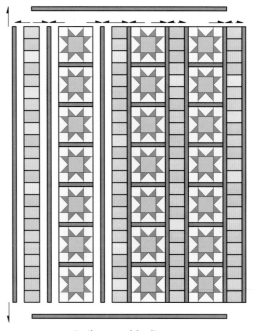

Quilt assembly diagram

4. Referring to "Adding the Borders" (page 12), use the 5½" x 42" green floral strips to make the side, top, and bottom borders for the quilt. Pin and sew the borders to the quilt. Press the seams toward the border.

FINISHING THE QUILT

Refer to "Finishing Techniques" on page 13 as needed to complete the following steps.

1. Layer, baste, and quilt your quilt. The Star blocks in the quilt on page 64 were machine quilted in a grid pattern. A scroll motif was quilted along the pieced sashing rows, and the outer border was quilted with a swag design.

2. Bind the quilt using the 2½"-wide pink-and-green plaid bias (or straight-grain) strips.

Quilt plan

Pieced, appliquéd, and quilted by Cindy Lammon.

Finished Quilt: 56½" x 74½"

My Secret Garden

Like a garden filled with a variety of flowers and plants, this quilt—with a variety of blocks—is not only fun to create, but also charming to look at. To make the pattern easy to follow, the cutting and assembly instructions for each section are grouped together, allowing you to work on one section at a time without getting your fabric patches mixed up.

MATERIALS

All yardages are based on 42"-wide fabric unless otherwise noted. Fat quarters measure 18" x 21". There will be sufficient scraps from these fabrics to make the necessary appliqués.

1⅞ yards of cream tone-on-tone print for block backgrounds

1⅓ yards of dark pink floral print for blocks and outer border

1¼ yards *total* OR 5 fat quarters of assorted light pink prints for blocks*

1 yard *total* OR 4 fat quarters of assorted dark pink prints for blocks*

1 yard *total* OR 4 fat quarters of assorted yellow prints for blocks*

1 yard *total* OR 4 fat quarters of assorted light green prints for blocks*

¾ yard *total* OR 3 fat quarters of assorted dark green prints for blocks*

½ yard *each* of green print 1 and green print 2 for filler strips and checkerboards

½ yard of yellow print 1 for filler strips and checkerboards

⅓ yard of yellow print 2 for filler strips

¼ yard of green-and-pink striped fabric for filler strips

⅝ yard of green print for binding

4½ yards of backing fabric (vertical seam) OR 3½ yards (horizontal seam)

61" x 79" piece of batting

If you wish, you can use leftovers from the filler strip, checkerboard, border, and binding prints to supplement these fabrics.

CUTTING

To help you keep things organized, the cutting, piecing, and appliqué instructions for this quilt are presented in sections. Cutting for the outer borders and binding is specified below. Cut all strips across the width of the fabric unless otherwise noted.

From the dark pink floral print, cut:
7 strips, 4½" x 42"

From the green print for binding, cut:
7 strips, 2½" x 42"

CUTTING FOR SECTION 1

Section 1 consists of two Tulips in the Garden blocks, an appliquéd Vine and Leaf block, and filler strips.

Tulips in the Garden Blocks

From the cream tone-on-tone print, cut:
1 strip, 2⅞" x 42"; crosscut into 8 squares, 2⅞" x 2⅞".
    Cut each square once on the diagonal to make
    16 half-square triangles.
1 strip, 2½" x 42"; crosscut into 16 squares, 2½" x 2½".

From *each* of 2 assorted dark pink prints, cut:
4 squares, 2⅞" x 2⅞" (8 total); cut each square once
    on the diagonal to make 8 half-square triangles
    (16 total)
4 squares, 2½" x 2½" (8 total)

From one assorted yellow print, cut:
8 rectangles, 2½" x 4½"
12 squares, 2½" x 2½"

From one assorted light green print, cut:
1 square, 2½" x 2½"

From one assorted dark green print, cut:
1 square, 2½" x 2½"

From one assorted light pink print, cut:
8 rectangles, 2½" x 4½"
12 squares, 2½" x 2½"

Vine and Leaf Block

From the cream tone-on-tone print, cut:
1 strip, 5" x 29"

From the *bias* of one assorted dark green print, cut:
Enough ⅞"-wide strips to total 36"

Filler Strips

From green print 1, cut:
1 strip, 2½" x 18½"
1 strip, 2½" x 30½"

MAKING SECTION 1

Finished Size: 30" x 20"
Refer to "Quiltmaking Basics" (page 8) and "Hand-Appliqué Techniques" (page 17) as needed.

Tulips in the Garden Blocks

Finished Block: 14" x 14"
You will make two of these blocks in slightly different color variations.

1. With right sides together, sew a dark pink half-square triangle and a cream half-square triangle together along their long diagonal edges as shown; press. Make eight matching units.

Make 8.

2. Arrange two units from step 1, a 2½" cream square, and a 2½" matching dark pink square as shown. Sew the units and squares into rows; press. Sew the rows together; press. Make four.

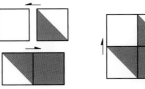

Make 4.

3. With right sides together, sew a 2½" cream square and a 2½" yellow square together as shown; press. Make four.

Make 4.

4. Arrange the units from step 2, the units from step 3, and the 2½" light green square as shown. Sew the units and square together into rows; press. Sew the rows together; press.

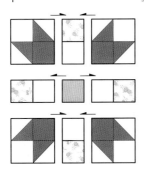 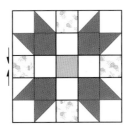

5. With right sides together, sew a 2½" light pink square between two 2½" x 4½" yellow rectangles as shown; press. Make four.

Make 4.

6. Sew a 2½" light pink square to each end of a unit from step 5; press. Make two.

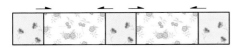

Make 2.

7. Arrange the unit from step 4, the units from step 5, and the units from step 6 as shown. Sew the unit from step 4 between the units from step 5; press. Sew the units from step 6 to the top and bottom; press.

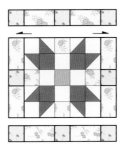 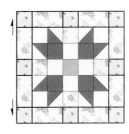

8. Repeat steps 1–7 to make a second block. Substitute the second dark pink half-square triangles and 2½" squares in steps 1 and 2. Substitute 2½" light pink squares for the 2½" yellow squares in step 3 and the 2½" dark green square for the 2½" light green square in step 4. In steps 5 and 6, substitute 2½" yellow squares for the 2½" light pink squares and 2½" x 4½" light pink rectangles for the 2½" x 4½" yellow rectangles as shown.

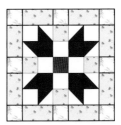

Vine and Leaf Block

Finished Block: 4" x 28"

1. Fold the 5" x 29" cream strip in half in both directions and finger-crease to establish centering lines. Use the pattern on page 91 to make a template for the vine placement guide. Center the template on the creased rectangle, aligning the long straight edge of the template with the horizontal crease as shown on page 72. Lightly trace the curved edge with a pencil. Flip the template to the opposite side of the crease,

matching it with the end of the first curve, and trace. Continue marking in this manner until you reach the end of the rectangle, and then repeat to mark the other end of the vine.

2. Referring to "Stems" (page 19), use the ⅞"-wide green bias strips to prepare a vine of the required length. Position and appliqué the vine on the curved line you marked in step 1.

3. Use pattern piece A on page 91 and assorted green scraps to prepare seven leaf appliqués. Appliqué the leaves to the block background, positioning them along the inside curves as shown. There are no reverse pattern pieces in this design.

4. Trim the block to 4½" x 28½", making sure to keep the appliqué centered in the block.

Assembling Section 1

1. Referring to the section 1 assembly diagram below, sew the two Tulips in the Garden blocks together side by side; press. Sew the appliquéd Vine and Leaf block to the bottom edge; press.

2. Sew the 2½" x 18½" green print 1 strip to the left edge of the unit from step 1; press. Sew the 2½" x 30½" green print 1 strip to the top; press. Set section 1 aside for now.

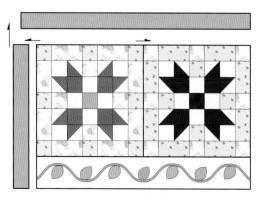

Section 1 assembly diagram

CUTTING FOR SECTION 2

Section 2 consists of one each of the Star Dahlia, Honey Bee, Rosebud, Flower Basket, and Hollyhock blocks, and filler strips.

Star Dahlia Block

From the cream tone-on-tone print, cut:
1 square, 3¼" x 3¼"; cut twice on the diagonal to make 4 quarter-square triangles
4 squares, 2⅞" x 2⅞"; cut each square once on the diagonal to make 8 half-square triangles
4 squares, 2½" x 2½"

From one assorted light green print, cut:
1 square, 3¼" x 3¼"; cut twice on the diagonal to make 4 quarter-square triangles

From one assorted light pink print, cut:
1 square, 5¼" x 5¼"; cut twice on the diagonal to make 4 quarter-square triangles
2 squares, 2⅞" x 2⅞"; cut each square once on the diagonal to make 4 half-square triangles

From one assorted dark pink print, cut:
2 squares, 4⅞" x 4⅞"; cut each square once on the diagonal to make 4 half-square triangles

From one assorted yellow print, cut:
1 square, 2½" x 2½"

Honey Bee Block

From one assorted dark pink print, cut:
5 squares, 2½" x 2½"

From one assorted light pink print, cut:
4 squares, 2½" x 2½"

From the cream tone-on-tone print, cut:
1 strip, 2½" x 42"; crosscut into:
     2 rectangles, 2½" x 6½"
     2 rectangles, 2½" x 10½"

Rosebud Block

From one assorted dark pink print, cut:
4 squares, 2⅜" x 2⅜"; cut each square once on the
    diagonal to make 8 half-square triangles
4 squares, 2" x 2"

From the cream tone-on-tone print, cut:
8 squares, 2⅜" x 2⅜"; cut each square once on the
    diagonal to make 16 half-square triangles
4 rectangles, 1½" x 5"

From one assorted light green print, cut:
4 squares, 2⅜" x 2⅜"; cut each square once on the
    diagonal to make 8 half-square triangles
8 squares, 2" x 2"
1 square, 1½" x 1½"

From one assorted dark green print, cut:
4 squares, 2" x 2"

From one assorted light pink print, cut:
4 squares, 2" x 2"

Flower Basket Block

From the cream tone-on-tone print, cut:
1 square, 6⅞" x 6⅞"; cut once on the diagonal to
    make 2 half-square triangles. You will have 1
    triangle left over.
1 square, 4⅞" x 4⅞"; cut once on the diagonal to
    make 2 half-square triangles. You will have 1
    triangle left over.
2 rectangles, 2½" x 6½"
4 squares, 2⅞" x 2⅞"; cut each square once on the
    diagonal to make 8 half-square triangles. You
    will have 1 triangle left over.

From one assorted dark green print, cut:
4 squares, 2⅞" x 2⅞"; cut each square once on the
    diagonal to make 8 half-square triangles. You
    will have 1 triangle left over.

From one assorted dark pink print, cut:
1 square, 6⅞" x 6⅞"; cut once on the diagonal to
    make 2 half-square triangles. You will have 1
    triangle left over.
1 square, 2⅞" x 2⅞"; cut once on the diagonal to
    make 2 half-square triangles

From one assorted light green print, cut:
2 squares, 8¼" x 8¼"; cut each square once on the
    diagonal to make 4 half-square triangles*

*These triangles are cut oversized; you will trim them
to size when the block is completed.*

Hollyhock Block

From one assorted yellow print, cut:

1 rectangle, 9" x 15"

From one assorted light or dark green print, cut:

1 strip, ⅞" x 12"

Filler Strip

From the green-and-pink striped fabric, cut:

4 strips, 1½" x 14½"

From yellow print 2, cut:

1 rectangle, 4½" x 14½"

MAKING SECTION 2

Finished Size: 30" x 24"

Refer to "Quiltmaking Basics" (page 8) and "Hand-Appliqué Techniques" (page 17) as needed.

Star Dahlia Block

Finished Block: 10" x 10"

1. With right sides together, sew a light green quarter-square triangle and a cream quarter-square triangle together along their short sides as shown; press. Make four. Sew a cream half-square triangle to each unit; press. Make four.

Make 4.

2. With right sides together, sew a light pink quarter-square triangle to each unit from step 1 as shown; press. Sew a dark pink half-square triangle to each unit; press. Make four.

Make 4.

3. With right sides together, sew a light pink half-square triangle and a cream half-square triangle together along their long diagonal edges as shown; press. Make four. Sew a 2½" cream square to each unit as shown; press.

Make 4.

4. Sew a unit from step 2 and step 3 together as shown; press. Make four.

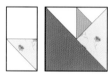 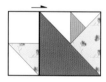

Make 4.

5. Place one unit from step 4 along the top edge of the 2½" yellow square as shown. With right sides together, and beginning from the outside raw edge, sew the unit and square together, stopping ½" from the opposite corner of the square; press.

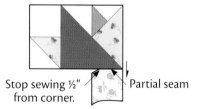

Stop sewing ½" from corner.   Partial seam

6. With right sides together, sew units from step 4 to the right, bottom, and left edges of the unit from step 5 as shown, in each case sewing

the complete seam and pressing each seam as it is sewn. Finish sewing the partial seam you stitched in step 5; press.

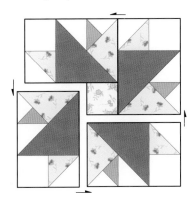

Honey Bee Block

Finished Block: 10" x 10"

1. Arrange and sew the five 2½" dark pink squares and four 2½" light pink squares as shown. Sew the squares together into rows; press. Sew the rows together; press. Sew 2½" x 6½" cream rectangles to the sides of the unit; press. Sew 2½" x 10½" cream rectangles to the top and bottom; press.

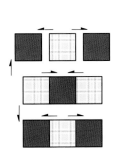 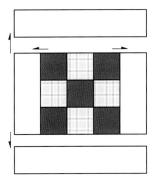

2. Use pattern piece B on page 91 and assorted green scraps to prepare 12 B appliqués. Appliqué three B pieces to each corner of the block as shown.

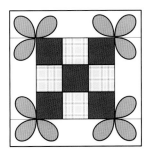

Rosebud Block

Finished Block: 10" x 10"

1. With right sides together, sew a dark pink half-square triangle and a cream half-square triangle together along their long diagonal edges as shown; press. Make eight. Repeat, substituting light green half-square triangles for the dark pink half-square triangles; press. Make eight.

Make 8 of each.

2. Arrange two dark pink units and two light green units from step 1, one 2" dark green square, two 2" light green squares, one 2" dark pink square, and one 2" light pink square as shown. Sew the units and squares together into rows; press. Sew the rows together; press. Make four.

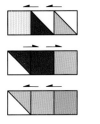

Make 4.

3. Arrange the four units from step 2, the four 1½" x 5" cream rectangles, and the 1½" light green square as shown. Sew the units, rectangles, and square together into rows; press. Sew the rows together; press.

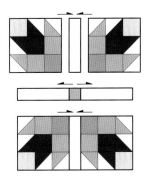 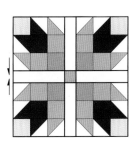

Flower Basket Block

Finished Block: 14" x 14"

1. With right sides together, sew a $2\frac{7}{8}$" cream half-square triangle and a $2\frac{7}{8}$" dark green half-square triangle together along their long diagonal edges as shown; press. Make seven. Sew the units together to make one row of three units and one row of four units; press.

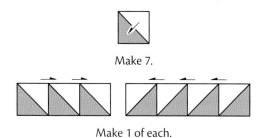

Make 7.

Make 1 of each.

2. Repeat step 1 to sew the $6\frac{7}{8}$" dark pink half-square triangle and the $6\frac{7}{8}$" cream half-square triangle together; press. Sew the two units from step 1 to adjacent sides of this new unit as shown; press.

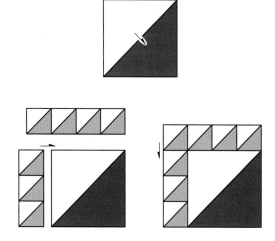

3. Sew a $2\frac{7}{8}$" dark pink half-square triangle to one end of a $2\frac{1}{2}$" x $6\frac{1}{2}$" cream rectangle; press. Make one of each, taking careful note of the placement of the triangles. Sew these units to adjacent sides of the unit from step 2 as shown;

press. Center and sew the $4\frac{7}{8}$" cream half-square triangle to the bottom edge of the unit; press.

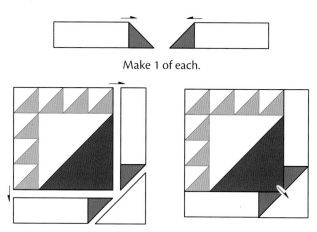

Make 1 of each.

4. Center and sew a light green half-square triangle to opposite sides of the unit from step 3; press. Repeat to sew the remaining two light green half-square triangles to the remaining sides of the unit; press.

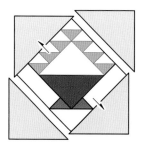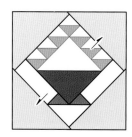

5. Use pattern pieces C–F on page 91 and assorted pink and yellow scraps to prepare one each of flower appliqué pieces C–E, and assorted green scraps to prepare two of leaf appliqué F. There are no reverse pattern pieces in this design.

Appliqué the flower and leaves to the basket as shown.

Appliqué placement diagram

6. Trim the block to 14½" x 14½", making sure to keep the basket centered in the block.

Hollyhock Block

Finished Block: 8" x 14"

1. Fold the 9" x 15" yellow rectangle in half in both directions and finger-crease to establish centering lines.

2. Referring to "Stems" (page 19), use the ⅞" x 12" green strip to prepare a stem. Center the stem on the vertical crease in the background block, aligning the bottom raw edge of the stem with the bottom raw edge of the block. Appliqué the stem.

3. Use pattern pieces G–M on page 92 and assorted pink and yellow scraps to prepare flower appliqué pieces G–I and M, and assorted green scraps to prepare leaf appliqués J and K and grass appliqué L. The patterns tell you how many to cut of each piece, and identify any reversed pieces. Appliqué the flowers and leaves to the block, placing them whimsically as shown. Appliqué piece L along the bottom edge

of the block, turning under the top edge of the shape only.

Appliqué placement diagram

4. Trim the block to 8½" x 14½", making sure to keep the appliqué centered in the block.

Assembling Section 2

Referring to the section 2 assembly diagram below, arrange and sew the Star Dahlia, Honey Bee, and Rosebud blocks together side by side; press. Arrange and sew the 1½" x 14½" striped strips, the 4½" x 14½" yellow print 2 rectangle, the Flower Basket block, and the Hollyhock block together as shown; press. Sew the two units together; press. Set section 2 aside for now.

Section 2 assembly diagram

CUTTING FOR SECTION 3

Section 3 consists of one each of the Sunshine, Birds in the Air, and Bird's Nest blocks, an appliquéd Bird block, and checkerboard, strip-pieced, and plain filler strips.

MEASURING TIP!

If you're having trouble finding the ¹⁄₁₆" markings, it's because most rotary-cutting rulers don't have them. To measure in increments of 16ths, position the edge of your fabric halfway between the appropriate ⅛" markings. For example: the ¹³⁄₁₆" line falls right between the ¾" and ⅞" lines on the ruler. It's a small space, so you can definitely eyeball it.

Sunshine Block

From the cream tone-on-tone print, cut:

1 strip, 2⅛" x 42"; crosscut into 12 squares, 2⅛" x 2⅛".
    Cut each square once on the diagonal to make
    24 half-square triangles.*

4 squares, 1¾" x 1¾"

From one assorted yellow print, cut:

12 squares, 2⅛" x 2⅛"; cut each square once on the
    diagonal to make 24 half-square triangles*

From a second assorted yellow print, cut:

2 squares, 4⅝" x 4⅝"; cut each square once on the
    diagonal to make 4 half-square triangles

From a third assorted yellow print, cut:

1 square, 5¹³⁄₁₆" x 5¹³⁄₁₆"

*Before cutting these pieces, read "Improve Your
    Accuracy!" above right.*

IMPROVE YOUR ACCURACY!

The small half-square triangles for the Sunshine block will be sewn into half-square-triangle units that—when sewn into a row—*must* fit the block's center square. For improved accuracy, you may want to cut the triangles oversized. To do so, cut the squares 2½" (rather than 2⅛") and then cut each square once on the diagonal.

When the triangles are pieced, trim the resulting half-square-triangle units to the exact size: 1¾". To do this, align the 45° diagonal line on a small square ruler over the seam line, and the 1¾" marking on the ruler within the lower-left corner of the unit to be trimmed. Trim the first two sides of the unit, rotate the unit, and trim the remaining two sides.

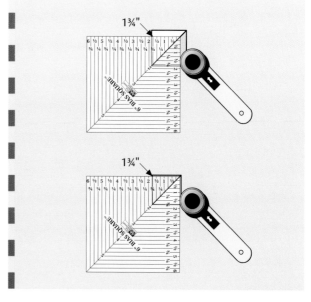

Birds in the Air Block

From one assorted dark green print, cut:

3 squares, 2⅞" x 2⅞"; cut each square once on the diagonal to make 6 half-square triangles. You will have 1 triangle left over.

1 square, 4½" x 4½"

From one assorted yellow print, cut:

3 squares, 2⅞" x 2⅞"; cut each square once on the diagonal to make 6 half-square triangles. You will have 1 triangle left over.

From the dark pink floral print, cut:

2 squares, 8" x 8"; cut each square once on the diagonal to make 4 half-square triangles*

These triangles are cut oversized; you will trim them to size when the block is completed.

Bird Block

From the cream tone-on-tone print, cut:

1 rectangle, 9" x 11"

From the *bias* of one assorted dark green print, cut:

1 strip, ⅞" x 6½"

Bird's Nest Block

From one assorted light pink print, cut:

2 squares, 2⅞" x 2⅞"; cut each square once on the diagonal to make 4 half-square triangles

2 squares, 4⅞" x 4⅞"; cut each square once on the diagonal to make 4 half-square triangles

From the cream tone-on-tone print, cut:

6 squares, 2⅞" x 2⅞"; cut each square once on the diagonal to make 12 half-square triangles

3 squares, 3¼" x 3¼"; cut each square twice on the diagonal to make 12 quarter-square triangles

6 squares, 1⅞" x 1⅞"; cut each square once on the diagonal to make 12 half-square triangles

From one assorted dark green print, cut:

8 squares, 1¹⁵⁄₁₆" x 1¹⁵⁄₁₆"

From one assorted yellow print, cut:

1 square, 1¹⁵⁄₁₆" x 1¹⁵⁄₁₆"

Checkerboard Border

From green print 1, cut:

3 strips, 2½" x 42"

From yellow print 1, cut:

3 strips, 2½" x 42"

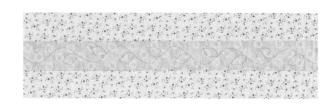

Strip-Pieced and Plain Filler Strips

From green print 1, cut:
1 strip, 2½" x 32½"

From green print 2, cut:
1 strip, 2½" x 38½"

From yellow print 2, cut:
2 strips, 2½" x 32½"

MAKING SECTION 3

Finished Size: 18" x 44"

Refer to "Quiltmaking Basics" (page 8) and "Hand-Appliqué Techniques" (page 17) as needed.

Sunshine Block

Finished Block: 10" x 10"

1. With right sides together, sew a cream half-square triangle and a first yellow half-square triangle along their long diagonal edges as shown; press. Make 24. If you cut these pieces oversized, refer to the box "Improve Your Accuracy!" (page 78) and trim the units now to measure 1¾" square.

Make 24.

2. Sew six units from step 1 together, turning the triangles as shown. To reduce bulk, press the seam allowances open. Make four.

Make 4.

3. Sew a 1¾" cream square to each end of a unit from step 2 as shown press. Make two.

Make 2.

4. Center and sew a second yellow half-square triangle to opposite sides of the 5¹³⁄₁₆" third yellow square; press. Repeat to sew the remaining two second yellow half-square triangles to the remaining sides of the square; press.

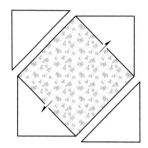 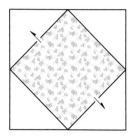

5. Sew the units from step 2 to the sides of the unit from step 4 as shown; press. Sew the units from step 3 to the top and bottom; press.

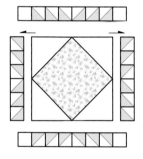 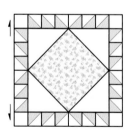

Birds in the Air Block

Finished Block: 10" x 10"

1. With right sides together, sew a dark green half-square triangle and a yellow half-square triangle along their long diagonal edges as shown; press. Make five. Sew the units together to make one row of two units and one row of three units; press.

  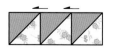

Make 5.   Make 1 of each.

2. Sew the two-square unit from step 1 to the top edge of the 4½" dark green square as shown; press. Sew the three-square unit from step 1 to the right edge; press.

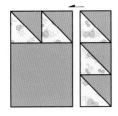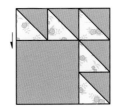

3. Center and sew a dark pink floral half-square triangle to opposite sides of the unit from step 2 as shown; press. Repeat to sew the remaining two dark pink triangles to the remaining sides of the unit; press.

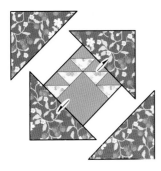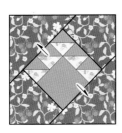

4. Trim the block to 10½" x 10½", making sure to keep the design centered in the block.

Bird Block

Finished Block: 10" x 8"

1. Fold the 11" x 9" cream rectangle in half in both directions and finger-crease to establish centering lines.

2. Referring to "Stems" (page 19), use the ⅞" x 6½" green bias strip to prepare a stem.

3. Use pattern pieces O–T on page 93 and assorted pink and yellow scraps to prepare one each of bird (O–Q) and flower (R and S) appliqués and three berry appliqués (T), and use assorted green scraps to prepare three leaf appliqués (N). The patterns identify any

reversed pieces. Appliqué the stem, bird, flowers, berries, and leaves to the block as shown.

Appliqué placement diagram

4. Trim the block to 10½" x 8½", making sure to keep the appliqué centered in the block.

Bird's Nest Block

Finished Block: 10" x 10"

1. With right sides together, sew a 2⅞" light pink half-square triangle and a 2⅞" cream half-square triangle together along their long diagonal edges as shown; press. Make four. Sew a 2⅞" cream half-square triangle to adjacent sides of each unit as shown; press. Make four. Sew a 4⅞" light pink half-square triangle to each unit; press. Make four.

Make 4.

Make 4.

2. Sew a cream quarter-square triangle to one side of a 1¹⁵⁄₁₆" dark green square as shown; press. Make four and then sew these units together to make two pairs.

Make 4.　　　Make 2.

3. Sew 1⅞" cream half-square triangles to the outside corners of each unit from step 2 as shown; press. Make two.

Make 2.

4. Sew cream quarter-square triangles to the remaining 1⁵⁄₁₆" dark green squares and to the 1⁵⁄₁₆" yellow square as shown; press. Arrange and sew the units together; press. Sew 1⅞" cream half-square triangles to the outside corners of the unit; press.

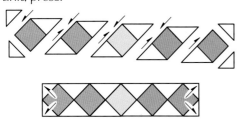

5. Arrange the four units from step 1, the two units from step 3, and the unit from step 4 as shown. Sew the units together into rows; press. Sew the rows together; press.

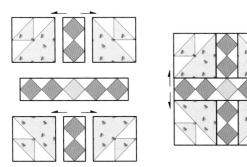

Checkerboard

1. With right sides together, sew a 2½"-wide yellow print 1 strip between two 2½"-wide green print 1 strips along their long edges to make a strip set as shown; press. Crosscut the strip set into 12 segments, each 2½".

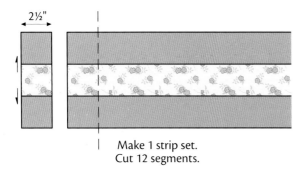

Make 1 strip set.
Cut 12 segments.

2. Repeat step 1 to sew a 2½"-wide green print 1 strip between two 2½"-wide yellow print 1 strips to make a strip set; press. Crosscut the strip set into 12 segments, each 2½".

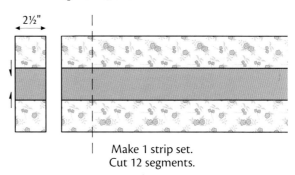

Make 1 strip set.
Cut 12 segments.

3. Arrange and sew two segments from step 1 and a segment from step 2 together as shown; press. Label this unit A.

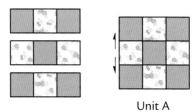

Unit A

4. Arrange and sew five segments from step 2 and four segments from step 1, alternating them as shown; press. Label this unit B.

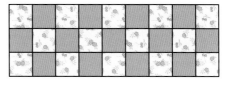

Unit B

5. Arrange and sew six segments from step 1 and six segments from step 2, alternating them as shown; press. Label this unit C, and set this aside for section 4.

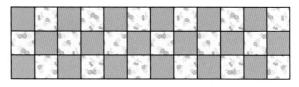

Unit C

Strip-Pieced Filler Strip

With right sides together, sew a 2½" x 32½" green print 2 strip between two 2½" x 32½" yellow print 2 strips along their long edges to make a strip set as shown; press.

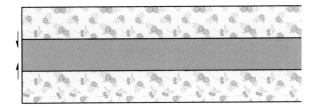

Assembling Section 3

1. Referring to the section 3 assembly diagram below, arrange and sew the Sunshine, Birds in the Air, Bird, and Bird's Nest blocks together to make a vertical row as shown; press. Sew the 2½" x 38½" medium green 1 strip to the left edge of the unit; press.

2. Sew checkerboard unit A to one end of the strip-pieced filler unit; press. Sew this unit to the right edge of the unit from step 1; press.

3. Sew checkerboard unit B to the top edge of the unit from step 2; press. Set section 3 aside for now.

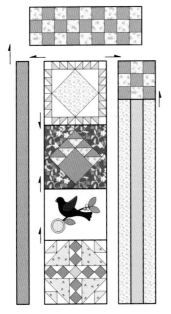

Section 3 assembly diagram

CUTTING FOR SECTION 4

Section 4 consists of one each of the Garden of Eden block and Garden Path blocks, the checkerboard unit left over from section 3, and a filler strip.

Garden of Eden Block

From the cream tone-on-tone print, cut:
1 strip, 2½" x 42"; crosscut into 12 squares, 2½" x 2½"

From one assorted light green print, cut:
4 squares, 2½" x 2½"

From one assorted yellow print, cut:
4 squares, 4½" x 4½"

From one assorted dark green print, cut:
4 squares, 2½" x 2½"

From one assorted light pink print, cut:
5 squares, 2½" x 2½"

From a second assorted light pink print, cut:
2 strips, 1½" x 10½"
2 strips, 1½" x 12½"

Garden Path Block

From the cream tone-on-tone print, cut:

4 rectangles, 1¹⁵⁄₁₆" x 3⁵⁄₁₆"

2 squares, 2⅞" x 2⅞"; cut each square once on the diagonal to make 4 half-square triangles

8 squares, 1¹⁵⁄₁₆" x 1¹⁵⁄₁₆"

From one assorted light green print, cut:

4 squares, 3⁵⁄₁₆" x 3⁵⁄₁₆"

From one assorted light pink print, cut:

3 squares, 3¼" x 3¼"; cut each square twice on the diagonal to make 12 quarter-square triangles

1 square, 3⁵⁄₁₆" x 3⁵⁄₁₆"

From one assorted yellow print, cut:

4 squares, 1¹⁵⁄₁₆" x 1¹⁵⁄₁₆"

From one assorted dark pink print, cut:

2 strips, 1½" x 10½"

2 strips, 1½" x 12½"

Filler Strip

From yellow print 1, cut:

1 rectangle, 4½" x 24½"

MAKING SECTION 4

Finished Size: 24" x 22"

Refer to "Quiltmaking Basics" (page 8) and "Hand-Appliqué Techniques" (page 17) as needed.

Garden of Eden Block

Finished Block: 12" x 12"

1. Referring to "Folded Triangles" (page 12), use your preferred marker and a ruler to draw a

line from corner to corner on the wrong side of each 2½" cream square and 2½" light green square. With right sides together, place a marked cream square and a marked light green square on opposite corners of a 4½" yellow square, noting the direction of the drawn line. Sew on the diagonal line; press. Trim the excess fabric, leaving a ¼" seam allowance. Repeat to sew a 2½" cream square to the remaining corners; press. Make four.

Make 4.

2. With right sides together, sew a 2½" light pink square and a 2½" dark green square together as shown; press. Make four.

Make 4.

3. Sew the remaining 2½" light pink square between two units from step 2; press.

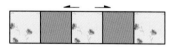

Make 1.

4. Arrange the four units from step 1, the two units from step 2, and the unit from step 3 as shown. Sew the units into rows; press. Sew the rows together; press.

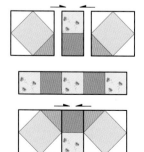 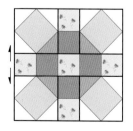

5. Sew the 1½" x 10½" light pink strips to the sides of the unit from step 4 as shown; press. Sew the 1½" x 12½" light pink strips to the top and bottom; press.

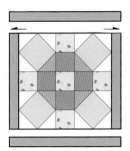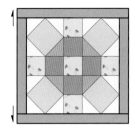

Garden Path Block

Finished Block: 12" x 12"

1. Sew a 1¹⁵⁄₁₆" x 3⁵⁄₁₆" cream rectangle to one side of a 3⁵⁄₁₆" light green square as shown; press. Center and sew a cream half-square triangle to the opposite side of the light green square; press. Make four.

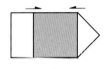

Make 4.

2. Sew a light pink quarter-square triangle to a 1¹⁵⁄₁₆" cream square as shown; press. Make eight. Sew a 1¹⁵⁄₁₆" yellow square to four of these units; press.

Make 8.   Make 4.

3. Arrange one of each unit from step 2 and a light pink quarter-square triangle as shown. Sew the units and triangle together; press. Make four.

Make 4.

4. Arrange the four units from step 1, the four units from step 3, and a 3⁵⁄₁₆" light pink square as shown. Sew the units and square together into diagonal sections; press. Sew the sections together; press.

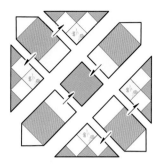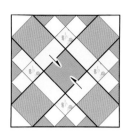

5. Sew the 1½" x 10½" dark pink strips to the sides of the unit from step 4 as shown; press. Sew the 1½" x 12½" dark pink strips to the top and bottom; press.

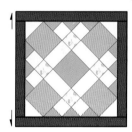

Assembling Section 4

Referring to the section 4 assembly diagram below, sew the Garden of Eden and Garden Path blocks together side by side; press. Sew the 4½" x 24½" yellow print 1 rectangle to the top of the unit; press. Sew checkerboard unit C, which you set aside from section 3, to the bottom; press.

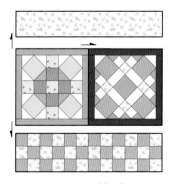

Section 4 assembly diagram

CUTTING FOR SECTION 5

Section 5 consists of a Flower block, an appliquéd Butterfly block, a Brick Wall block with appliquéd vines and leaves, a Birdhouse block, and filler strips.

Flower Block

From the cream tone-on-tone print, cut:
1 strip, 1⅜" x 42"; crosscut into 12 squares, 1⅜" x 1⅜"

From one assorted yellow print, cut:
4 squares, 1⅜" x 1⅜"

From one assorted dark pink print, cut:
4 squares, 3½" x 3½"

Butterfly Block

From the cream tone-on-tone print, cut:
1 square, 5" x 5"

From one assorted light green print, cut:
2 rectangles, 1½" x 4½"
2 rectangles, 1½" x 6½"

Brick Wall Block

From the assorted light pink prints, cut *a total of:*
18 rectangles, 2½" x 4½"
6 squares, 2½" x 2½"

From the *bias* of the assorted light and dark green prints, cut *a total of:*
3 strips, ⅞" x 18"

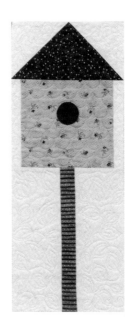

Birdhouse Block

From the cream tone-on-tone print, cut:
2 squares, 4½" x 4½"
2 rectangles, 1¼" x 6½"
2 rectangles, 4" x 10½"

From one assorted dark pink print, cut:
1 rectangle, 4½" x 8½"

From one assorted light pink print, cut:

1 rectangle, 7" x 6½"

From one assorted dark green print, cut:

1 strip, 1½" x 10½"

Filler Strips

From green print 2, cut:

2 strips, 2½" x 20½"

1 strip, 2½" x 24½"

MAKING SECTION 5

Finished Size: 24" x 20"

Refer to "Quiltmaking Basics" (page 8) and "Hand-Appliqué Techniques" (page 17) as needed.

Flower Block

Finished Block: 6" x 6"

1. Referring to "Folded Triangles" (page 12), use your preferred marker and a ruler to draw a line from corner to corner on the wrong side of each 1⅜" cream square and 1⅜" yellow square. With right sides together, place a marked cream square on three corners and a marked yellow square on the remaining corner of a 3½" dark pink square, noting the direction of the drawn line. Sew on the diagonal lines; press. Trim the excess fabric, leaving a ¼" seam allowance. Make four.

Make 4.

2. Arrange the four units from step 1, with the yellow triangles meeting in the center as shown. Sew the units into rows; press. Sew the rows together; press.

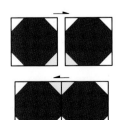 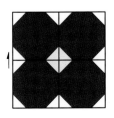

Butterfly Block

Finished Block: 6" x 6"

1. Fold the 5" cream square in half in both directions and finger-crease to establish centering lines.

2. Use pattern pieces U–W on page 93 and assorted pink scraps to prepare one each of the butterfly wing (U and V) and body (W) appliqués. There are no reversed pieces in this design. Appliqué the butterfly to the block as shown in the diagram following step 4.

3. Trim the block to 4½" x 4½", making sure to keep the appliqué centered in the block.

4. Sew the 1½" x 4½" light green strips to the sides of the appliqué block as shown; press. Sew the 1½" x 6½" light green strips to the top and bottom; press.

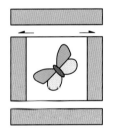 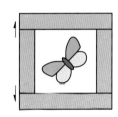

Brick Wall Block

Finished Block: 12" x 14"

1. Arrange and sew together three 2½" x 4½" assorted light pink rectangles as shown; press. Make four.

Make 4.

2. Arrange and sew together two 2½" assorted light pink squares and two 2½" x 4½" assorted light pink rectangles as shown; press. Make three.

Make 3.

3. Arrange and sew together the rows from steps 1 and 2, alternating them as shown; press.

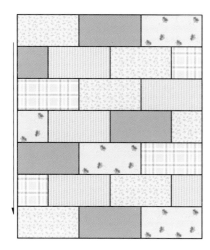

4. Referring to "Stems" (page 19), use the ⅞" x 18" green bias strips to prepare three stems. Curve one stem down the center of the brick wall unit from step 3 and place a remaining stem on the left and right sides as shown in the diagram following step 5. Appliqué the stems in place.

5. Use pattern piece X on page 93 and the assorted green scraps to prepare 28 leaf appliqués. There are no reverse pattern pieces in this design. Appliqué the leaves to the block background, placing them whimsically along the three stems as shown.

Appliqué placement diagram

Birdhouse Block

Finished Block: 8" x 20"

1. Referring to "Folded Triangles" (page 12), use your preferred marker and a ruler to draw a line from corner to corner on the wrong side of each 4½" cream square. With right sides together, place a marked cream square on one end of the 4½" x 8½" dark pink rectangle, noting the direction of the drawn line. Sew on the diagonal line; press. Trim the excess fabric, leaving a ¼" seam allowance. Repeat to sew a 4½" cream square to the opposite end of the rectangle; press.

2. Sew the 7" x 6½" light pink rectangle between two 1¼" x 6½" cream rectangles as shown; press. Use pattern piece Y on page 93 and a small dark pink scrap to make a birdhouse hole appliqué. Center and appliqué the circle 1¾" from the roof of the birdhouse as shown.

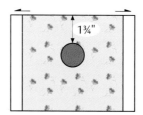

1¾"

3. Sew the 1½" x 10½" dark green strip between two 4" x 10½" cream rectangles as shown; press.

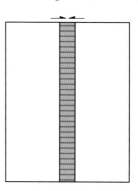

4. Arrange and sew the units from steps 1–3 together as shown; press.

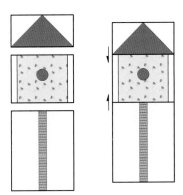

Assembling Section 5

1. Referring to the section 5 assembly diagram below, sew the Flower block and the Butterfly block together side by side; press. Sew this unit to the top of the Brick Wall block; press.

2. Sew the Birdhouse block to the right edge of the unit from step 1.

3. Sew the unit from step 2 between two 2½" x 20½" green print 2 strips; press. Sew the 2½" x 24½" green print 2 strip to the bottom; press.

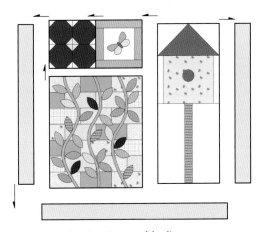

Section 5 assembly diagram

ASSEMBLING THE QUILT TOP

1. Referring to the quilt assembly diagram below, arrange sections 1–5 as shown. Sew sections 1 and 2 together; press. Sew section 3 to the right edge of sections 1-2; press. Sew sections 4 and 5 together; press. Sew sections 4-5 to the bottom edge of sections 1-2-3; press.

Quilt assembly diagram

2. Referring to "Adding the Borders" (page 12), use the 4½"-wide dark pink floral strips to make the side, top, and bottom outer borders for the quilt. Pin and sew the borders to the quilt. Press the seams toward the border.

FINISHING THE QUILT

Refer to "Finishing Techniques" (page 13) as needed to complete the following steps.

1. Layer, baste, and quilt your quilt. The quilt on page 68 was machine quilted by stitching in the ditch around most of the pieced shapes. The appliqué backgrounds were closely stippled and various garden-themed motifs—such as flowers, leaves, and butterflies—were quilted in the open areas. The checkerboards were crosshatched and the borders were quilted using a swag motif.

2. Bind the quilt using the 2½" x 42" green strips.

Quilt plan

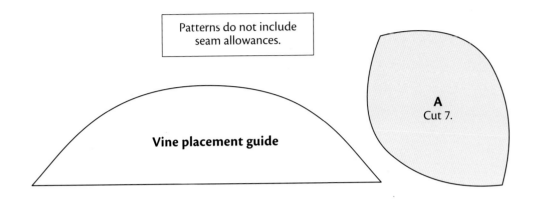

Patterns do not include
seam allowances.

Vine placement guide

A
Cut 7.

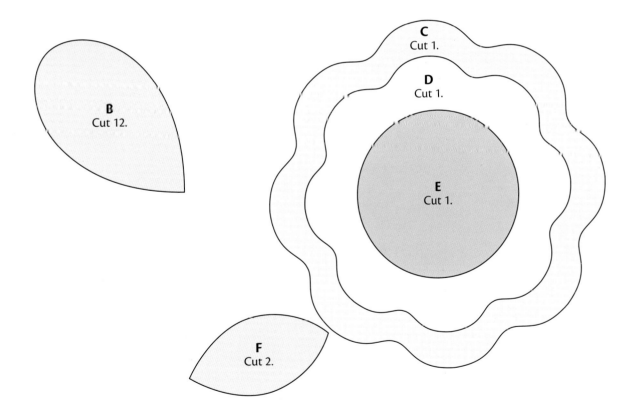

B
Cut 12.

C
Cut 1.

D
Cut 1.

E
Cut 1.

F
Cut 2.

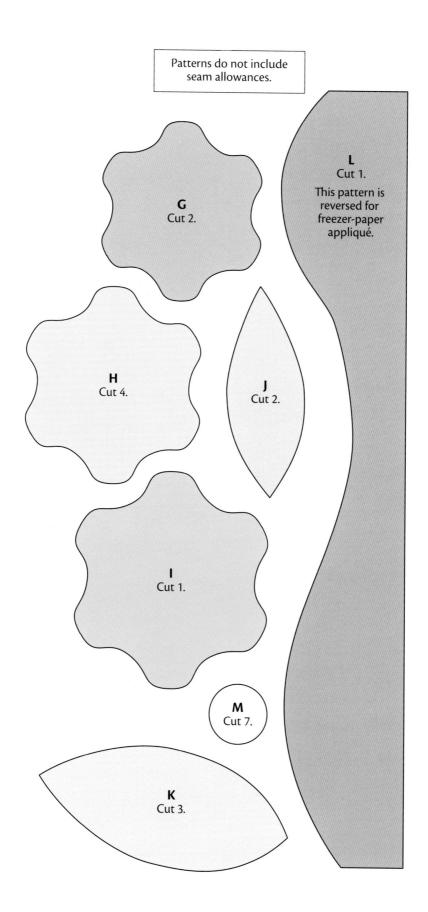

Patterns do not include seam allowances.

G
Cut 2.

L
Cut 1.

This pattern is reversed for freezer-paper appliqué.

H
Cut 4.

J
Cut 2.

I
Cut 1.

M
Cut 7.

K
Cut 3.

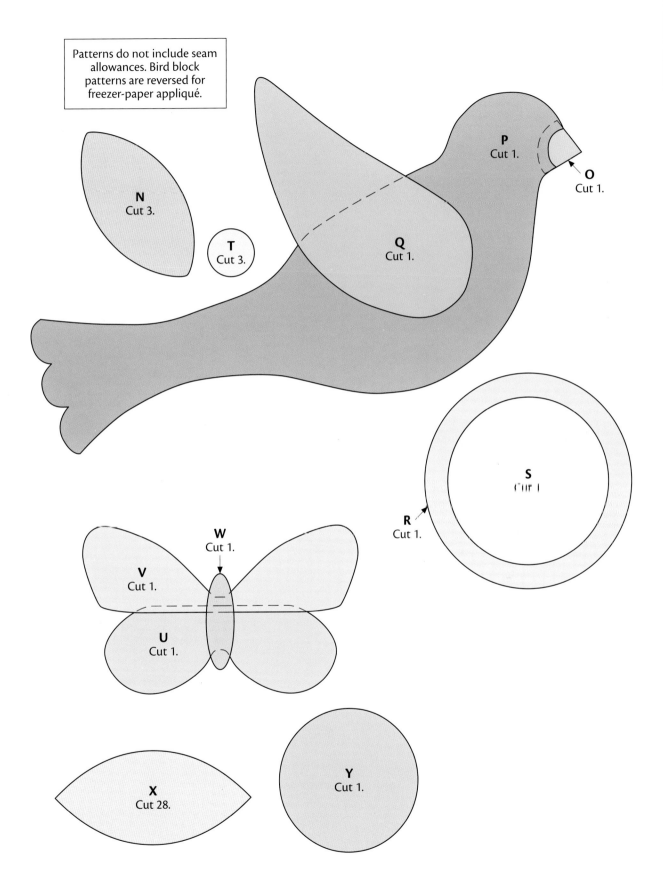

Patterns do not include seam allowances. Bird block patterns are reversed for freezer-paper appliqué.

N
Cut 3.

T
Cut 3.

P
Cut 1.

O
Cut 1.

Q
Cut 1.

S
Cut 1.

R
Cut 1.

W
Cut 1.

V
Cut 1.

U
Cut 1.

X
Cut 28.

Y
Cut 1.

About the Author

CINDY LAMMON took her first quilting class in 1981 and was hooked immediately! Since then, her love of fabric, pattern, and design has developed into a passion for all quilting techniques. She enjoys machine piecing and machine quilting, but also takes pleasure in the peacefulness of hand quilting and hand appliqué. The design process seems to come naturally because of her love for art and, believe it or not, geometry! She finds that quilting provides a wonderful creative outlet, but more important, it also offers the opportunity for many great friendships with fellow quilters. In addition to quilting, Cindy loves to garden, and during the spring and summer months she is often torn between these two favorite pursuits.

Cindy loves to teach quiltmaking techniques to others and enjoys the excitement in a new quilter's eyes. She's been teaching for over 15 years in the St. Louis, Missouri, area and likes to encourage beginners to dare to try something new! She currently works and teaches several classes at Raspberry Patch Quilt Shop in the St. Charles County area of Missouri.

Cindy lives outside of St. Louis with her husband, Mike, and is very grateful to spend her days doing something she loves.

NEW AND BESTSELLING TITLES FROM

America's Best-Loved Craft & Hobby Books®
America's Best-Loved Knitting Books®

America's Best-Loved Quilt Books®

APPLIQUÉ
Adoration Quilts
Beautiful Blooms—*New!*
Cutting-Garden Quilts
Favorite Quilts from Anka's Treasures
Mimi Dietrich's Favorite Applique Quilts
Sunbonnet Sue and Scottie Too

FOCUS ON WOOL
The Americana Collection
Needle-Felting Magic
Needle Felting with Cotton and Wool—*New!*
Simply Primitive

GENERAL QUILTMAKING
Bits and Pieces
Bound for Glory
Calendar Kids
Charmed
Christmas with Artful Offerings
Colorful Quilts
Comfort and Joy
Cool Girls Quilt
Creating Your Perfect Quilting Space
A Dozen Roses
Fig Tree Quilts: Houses
**Follow-the-Line Quilting Designs
      Volume Three**—*New!*
The Little Box of Quilter's Chocolate Desserts
Points of View
Positively Postcards
Prairie Children and Their Quilts
Quilt Revival
Quilter's Block-a-Day Calendar
Quilter's Happy Hour—*New!*
Quilting in the Country
Sensational Sashiko
Simple Seasons
Simple Seasons Recipe Cards
Simple Traditions
Skinny Quilts and Table Runners—*New!*
Twice Quilted
Young at Heart Quilts

LEARNING TO QUILT
Color for the Terrified Quilter
Happy Endings, Revised Edition
Let's Quilt!
Your First Quilt Book (or it should be!)

PAPER PIECING
300 Paper-Pieced Quilt Blocks
Easy Machine Paper Piecing
Paper-Pieced Mini Quilts
Show Me How to Paper Piece
Showstopping Quilts to Foundation Piece
Spellbinding Quilts

PIECING
40 Fabulous Quick-Cut Quilts
Better by the Dozen
Big 'n Easy
Clever Quarters, Too
Copy Cat Quilts—*New!*
Maple Leaf Quilts—*New!*
Mosaic Picture Quilts
New Cuts for New Quilts
Nine by Nine
Quilts on the Double—*New!*
Ribbon Star Quilts—*New!*
Sew Fun, Sew Colorful Quilts
Sew One and You're Done
Snowball Quilts
Square Deal
Sudoku Quilts
Wheel of Mystery Quilts

QUILTS FOR BABIES & CHILDREN
Baby Wraps—*New!*
Even More Quilts for Baby
Lickety-Split Quilts for Little Ones
The Little Box of Baby Quilts
Quilts for Baby
Sweet and Simple Baby Quilts

SCRAP QUILTS
Nickel Quilts
Save the Scraps
Simple Strategies for Scrap Quilts

CRAFTS
101 Sparkling Necklaces
Art from the Heart
The Beader's Handbook
Card Design
Creative Embellishments
Crochet for Beaders
It's a Wrap
It's in the Details
The Little Box of Beaded Bracelets
      and Earrings
The Little Box of Beaded Necklaces
      and Earrings
Miniature Punchneedle Embroidery
A Passion for Punchneedle
Punchneedle Fun
Scrapbooking off the Page…and on
      the Wall
Sculpted Threads
Sew Sentimental
Stitched Collage—*New!*

KNITTING & CROCHET
365 Crochet Stitches a Year:
      Perpetual Calendar
365 Knitting Stitches a Year:
      Perpetual Calendar
A to Z of Knitting
Amigurumi World—*New!*
Crocheted Pursenalities
First Crochet
First Knits
Fun and Funky Crochet
Handknit Skirts
Kitty Knits—*New!*
The Knitter's Book of Finishing
      Techniques
Knitting Circles around Socks
Knitting with Gigi
The Little Box of Crocheted Throws
The Little Box of Knitted Throws
Modern Classics
More Sensational Knitted Socks
Pursenalities
Wrapped in Comfort

Our books are available at bookstores and your favorite craft,
fabric, and yarn retailers. If you don't see the title you're looking for,
visit us at **www.martingale-pub.com** or contact us at:

1-800-426-3126

International: 1-425-483-3313 • **Fax:** 1-425-486-7596 • **Email:** info@martingale-pub.com